# O Come, Let Us Adore Him- A Christmas Devotional

Joshua Rhoades

Published by Joshua Paul Rhoades, 2024.

While every precaution has been taken in the preparation of this book, the publisher assumes no responsibility for errors or omissions, or for damages resulting from the use of the information contained herein.

O COME, LET US ADORE HIM- A CHRISTMAS DEVOTIONAL

**First edition. October 26, 2024.**

Copyright © 2024 Joshua Rhoades.

ISBN: 979-8227977212

Written by Joshua Rhoades.

# Also by Joshua Rhoades

Courage Under Fire: David's Stand On The Battlefield
Jonah's Journey: Voices Of Redemption And Lessons In Obedience
The Furnace Of Faith: 12 Principles From The Heat Of Faith
Whispers of Hope: Inspiring Stories of Men's Prayers In Scripture
Frontier Legends: The Oregon Dream
Elijah: A Beacon Of Boldness
HOOK, LINE & SAVIOUR - Faith Reflections from Fishing
Driven By Faith: Motor Racing Inspired Christian Life
30 Day Devotional - Bold and Strong- Coffee Devotions for a Courageous
Christian Walk
Authentic Christianity: The Heart of Old Time Religion
Consider The Ant - God's Tiny Preachers
Flee Fornication: The Plea For Purity
Renewed Hope- How to Find Encouragement in God
Sounding The Call - The Voice of Conviction
The Altar - Where Heaven Meets Earth
The Bible's Battlefields- Timeless Lessons from Ancient Wars
The Sacred Art of Silence - How Silence Speaks in Scripture
Under Fire- The Sanctity of the Traditional Biblical Home
Who Is on the Lord's Side? A Call to Righteousness
What Is Truth? - From Skepticism to Submission
First and Goal- Faith and Football Fundamentals
From Dugout to Devotion- Spiritual Lessons from Baseball
Par for the Course- Faith and Fairways
The Believer's Pace- Tools for Running Life's Marathon
The Immutable Fortress- Security in God's Unchanging Nature
Biblical Bravery
Deer Stands and Devotions: A Hunter's Walk with God

Jesus Knows- Our Hearts, Our Responsibility

Restoration - Setting The Bone

Spiritual 911- God's Word for Life's Emergency's

The Freedom of Forgiveness

The Jezebel Effect - Ancient Manipulations Modern Lessons

The Shout That Stopped The Saviour

The Time Machine Chronicles: Old Testament Characters

Anchored In Truth Exploring The Depths of Psalm 119

Biblical Counsel on Anger

Proverbs' Portraits The Men God Mentions

Stumbling in the Dark - The Dangers of Alcohol

Guarding the Wicket Protecting Your Faith and Game

The Champion's Faith - Wrestling and Achieving Spiritual Victory

Scriptural Commands for Modern Times Living God's Word Today Volume 1

Scriptural Commands for Modern Times Living God's Word Today Volume 2

Scriptural Commands for Modern Times Living God's Word TodayVolume3

The Greatest Gift

A Christmas Journey of Faith

Daughter Of The King: Embracing Your Identity In Christ

Determination and Dedication Building Strong Faith As A Young Man

Walking Through Walls God's Power to Part the Storms of Life

David's Song Of Deliverance Praising God Through Every Storm

From Weakness to Warrior: Gideon's Transformation

Why Did Jesus Weep?

Living For God The Call To Be A Living Sacrifice

My Mind Is In A Fog What Do I Do?

Turning The Page Written By Grace

The Calling and Greatness of John the Baptist

For Such a Time Esther's Courageous Stand

From Brokenness To Beauty Written By The Pen of Grace

The Ultimate Guide to Massive Action- From Plans to Reality

A Heart Of Conviction

Serving In The Shadows

Repentance Revealed The Road Back To God

The Chief Sinner Meets The Chief Saviour Reflections On I Timothy 1:15

Answer The Call - 31 Days of Biblical Action
The Birthmark of the Believer
Reflections on Calvary's Cross
The Kingdom Builder Paul's Bold Proclamation of Christ
The Animal Of Pride
The Reach That Restores Christ Love For The Broken
Paul- The Many Roles of a Servant of Christ
Unshakeable Faith- 31 Days of Peace in God's Word
O Come, Let Us Adore Him- A Christmas Devotional

# Dedication

To you, dear reader,

As you hold this devotional in your hands, know that it is no coincidence that you have chosen to embark on this journey. This book, "O Come, Let Us Adore Him: A Christmas Devotional," is not just a collection of reflections; it is an invitation to step into a season of wonder, hope, and deep joy. It is my prayer that as you read through these pages, your heart will be touched, your spirit will be lifted, and you will find yourself drawing closer to the true reason for the season—Jesus Christ, our Saviour.

Christmas is often filled with the hustle and bustle of preparations, celebrations, and traditions. But amidst the twinkling lights, festive gatherings, and beautiful decorations, there is a deeper, quieter message waiting for you. It is a message of love so profound, a hope so enduring, and a joy so pure that it has the power to transform your heart. This is the heart of Christmas—God's love wrapped in swaddling clothes, lying in a manger, coming near to us so that we might know Him, love Him, and be changed by His presence.

My hope for you is that this devotional becomes a gentle guide, leading you to slow down, to take a moment of quiet reflection each day, and to rediscover the wonder of the Christmas story. I pray that as you read, you will find yourself not just remembering a story from long ago, but encountering a love that is alive and real today. Let these words remind you that Jesus did not just come for the world—He came for you. He sees you, knows you, and loves you with a love that is unchanging and unfailing.

May each reflection be a balm to your soul, a reminder of God's faithfulness, and a call to rest in His presence. Whether you are filled with the joy of the season or walking through a time of struggle, know that Jesus is with you. He is Emmanuel, "God with us," bringing peace to every storm, light to every dark place, and hope that shines even in the deepest valleys. As you read, may you feel His gentle presence surrounding you, comforting you, and filling you with His peace.

The true gift of Christmas is not found under a tree but in the love that was born for you over two thousand years ago. That love has not changed; it is as strong and powerful today as it was on that holy night in Bethlehem. My prayer is that you will allow yourself to be captivated by this love, that you will let it seep into every part of your being, and that you will be inspired to share it with those around you. For as much as Christmas is about receiving God's love, it is also about giving that love to a world in need.

As you journey through this devotional, may your heart be filled with adoration for the One who came to bring you life, peace, and joy. Let this be a season where your faith is renewed, your hope is restored, and your love for Christ is deepened. And when Christmas morning arrives, may you find yourself kneeling at the manger in your heart, filled with gratitude, wonder, and awe at the gift of Jesus.

Introduction
Chapter 1 - Promise of the Savior
Chapter 2 - Prophecy of Promised Peace
Chapter 3 - Prince of Peace
Chapter 4 - Perfect Providence in God's Plan
Chapter 5 - Path of Profound Humility
Chapter 6 – Purity of the Promised Plan
Chapter 7 - Proclamation of Promised Peace
Chapter 8 – Promise of Profound Joy
Chapter 9 – Prelude to Divine Glory
Chapter 10 – Pursuit of Divine Presence
Chapter 11 – Portrait of Persevering Faith
Chapter 12 – Partnership of Quiet Obedience
Chapter 13 – Pathway of Divine Light
Chapter 14 – Pursuit of Reverent Adoration
Chapter 15 – Presentation of Profound Devotion
Chapter 16 – Presence of Perpetual Love
Chapter 17 - Protective Providence of God
Chapter 18 – Precious Provision of Grace
Chapter 19 - Piercing Presence of Divine Light
Chapter 20 – Portrait of Pure Joy
Chapter 21 – Pastoral Compassion Personified
Chapter 22 – Provision of Spiritual Nourishment
Chapter 23 – Powerful Promise of Hope
Chapter 24 – Pledge of a New Beginning
Chapter 25 - Prince of Eternal Life
Chapter 26 – Profound Offering of Redemption
Chapter 27 - Perfect Grace
Chapter 28 – Passionate Love
Chapter 29 – Priceless Redemption
Chapter 30 - Perpetual Reign
Chapter 31 – Profound Promise

# Introduction

"O Come, Let Us Adore Him: A Christmas Devotional" opens its pages to guide us through a season of wonder, hope, and unparalleled love as we journey toward Christmas. This devotional invites us to do more than just observe the season—it encourages us to experience it deeply, to reflect on the true meaning of Christmas, and to adore the One whose birth changed everything. The title, "O Come, Let Us Adore Him" is more than a phrase; it's a call to every heart to find its place at the manger, to marvel at the gift of Jesus, and to let that marvel transform us. The Christmas story isn't just an old tale to remember once a year; it's a revelation of God's unchanging love and His purpose to redeem, restore, and give us hope that will last forever.

The idea of adoration goes beyond the surface level—it beckons us to come with reverence and awe, to approach the Christ child not as a distant figure but as Emmanuel, "God with us." The heart of Christmas is Jesus, and each page in this devotional is crafted to help us remember and treasure His love. In a world filled with busyness and distractions, it's easy to lose sight of why we celebrate. This devotional invites us to slow down, to quiet our hearts, and to prepare ourselves to truly encounter Jesus. Each day, we are reminded that Christmas is not about the outward festivities but about the inner joy of knowing that God came to us. He stepped down from heaven, clothed in humility, born into a manger to become the Savior of the world.

Throughout these 31 days, you will be invited to reflect on different aspects of the Christmas story, each one revealing a facet of God's love and His perfect plan. As you journey through this devotional, you'll see that Christmas is a story of promises fulfilled, of love poured out, and of peace brought into a world longing for hope. It's a story that shows us God's faithfulness from the beginning of time to the present day. With each reading, we are given a new perspective on the Christmas story, from the prophecy of the Messiah to the humble shepherds who were the first to witness the miracle, to the wise men who traveled far to bring their gifts and worship. Through these reflections, we are reminded that Jesus was born for all people, for every heart that longs to be loved and saved.

Adoring Christ at Christmas means recognizing that His coming changes everything. When we look at Jesus, born as a baby, we see God's great humility and His willingness to enter into our broken world to bring healing and redemption. The manger in Bethlehem was a simple place, yet it held the most precious gift we could ever receive—God's only Son. The humility of Christ's birth shows us that God meets us in our everyday lives, in our own humble places. He didn't come with fanfare or demand attention; He came in a way that allows each of us to come close, to be part of His story. And that's what this devotional is about—drawing closer to Jesus, allowing the Christmas story to touch our hearts in a way that makes His love real and alive.

As we enter into this devotional, let's remember that adoration is about love, gratitude, and surrender. Adoring Jesus means opening our hearts to the wonder of who He is and what He has done. It means allowing ourselves to be moved, to let our hearts be softened, and to recognize our deep need for a Savior. When we adore Him, we give Him the honor, praise, and love that He deserves. We come, not with perfect lives, but with open hearts, willing to receive the peace and joy that He offers. Each devotion in this book is designed to help you do just that—to turn your focus back to Jesus, to let His love fill you with hope, and to embrace the peace that only He can bring.

Christmas is about light breaking into darkness, about hope overcoming despair, and about love conquering fear. When we take the time to come and adore Him, we experience that light, that hope, and that love in a way that transforms us. The Christmas season often brings a mix of emotions; for some, it's a time of joy, while for others, it may bring feelings of loneliness or loss. Yet, the message of Christmas is for everyone. It's a reminder that God sees us, that He knows our hearts, and that He came to bring us His peace. Jesus came to be our friend, our Savior, and our guide. He came to bring us a love that endures and a joy that sustains us.

"O Come, Let Us Adore Him" is not just a devotional; it's an invitation to experience Christmas in a way that brings you closer to the heart of God. It's an opportunity to step away from the noise, to find moments of quiet reflection, and to let the story of Jesus' birth remind you of the depth of God's love. Each day, you'll be invited to look at the Christmas story with fresh eyes, to see how it speaks to your life, and to find the joy of knowing that you are part of God's great plan. Through these daily readings, may you find that Christmas is not just a celebration of an event that happened long ago but a reminder that Jesus is present with us today, bringing hope, peace, and joy.

This season, as you read through this devotional, may your heart be filled with awe and wonder. May you find comfort in knowing that God's love is personal, that He came for you, and that His promises are true. Let each reading be a moment to connect with the God who came to earth to save us, to experience His love anew, and to remember that we are never alone. When we come to adore Jesus, we come to the source of all that we need. We find a peace that is greater than any worry, a love that is deeper than any hurt, and a hope that cannot be shaken.

In "O Come, Let Us Adore Him," you are invited to embrace the beauty of Christmas and to let its message sink deep into your soul. May each devotion bring you closer to Jesus, and may this season of reflection fill you with a faith that carries you forward. As you open your heart to adore Him, may you feel the warmth of His love, the joy of His presence, and the peace of knowing that you are held by a Savior who came for you. Let this Christmas be a time of renewal, a time to celebrate the greatest gift of all—Jesus Christ, our Lord and Savior.

# Chapter 1 - Promise of the Savior

In "O Come, Let Us Adore Him: A Christmas Devotional," we begin our journey by celebrating the promise of the Savior, a promise that reaches deep into the heart of God's unchanging love for His people. This promise is more than mere words—it is the very assurance of hope for a world shrouded in darkness. When God, through the prophet Isaiah, declared, "Therefore the Lord himself shall give you a sign; Behold, a virgin shall conceive, and bear a son, and shall call his name Immanuel" (Isaiah 7:14), He revealed a love that is boundless and a grace that could never be earned but is freely given. This promise, long awaited by generations, fills every page of Scripture with expectation, reminding us that even when humanity stumbled, God had a plan to redeem, to rescue, and to restore. Imagine the anticipation that grew over centuries as people longed for the coming of the Messiah, waiting for the fulfillment of a promise spoken by God Himself. The birth of Christ was not just an event but the glorious fulfillment of a divine promise, a promise that God would dwell among us, that He would be with us, walk with us, and carry the weight of sin and sorrow that we could not bear alone.

This promise of a Savior is central to the heart of Christmas. It tells us that God, who created the heavens and the earth, looked down with compassion upon a broken world and chose to come close, to walk in our midst, and to become our Immanuel, God with us. It reminds us that, even before the foundation of the world, God had us in mind. He knew every pain, every fear, every failure we would face, and He prepared a way of salvation. In His faithfulness, He promised a Savior who would bear our burdens, and in the fullness of time, that promise took flesh. God's promise wasn't just about a future hope; it was about a present reality that would change the course of history. The promise of the Savior was so powerful that it filled prophets with visions of light in the darkness, and it stirred the hearts of people who clung to the hope of His coming. "The people that walked in darkness have seen a great light: they that dwell in the land of the shadow of death, upon them hath the light shined" (Isaiah 9:2). This light, this Savior, was coming to break every chain, lift every sorrow, and fill our hearts with a peace that surpasses all understanding.

The promise of the Savior is a testament to God's faithfulness. When God makes a promise, He keeps it. "For all the promises of God in him are yea, and in him Amen, unto the glory of God by us" (2 Corinthians 1:20). At Christmas, we see the beautiful, awe-inspiring fulfillment of this promise in the birth of Jesus. The Son of God came as a child, born to Mary, fulfilling every prophecy with perfect timing. His coming was not delayed, nor was it hurried; it was exactly as God had planned. Even when circumstances seemed impossible, even when hope appeared dim, God's promise stood firm. Mary, a young virgin, became the vessel through which this promise was brought to life. The angel said to her, "Fear not, Mary: for thou hast found favour with God. And, behold, thou shalt conceive in thy womb, and bring forth a son, and shalt call his name Jesus" (Luke 1:30-31). Mary's faithful response and trust in God's word made way for the promise to enter our world in the most extraordinary way.

God's promise of the Savior was not only a promise to Mary or to the people of Israel; it was a promise to all of us. Through Christ's birth, God extended His arms to a lost world, inviting each one of us to come and be part of His family. In Jesus, we find forgiveness, love, and new life. Christmas is a celebration of God's promise made personal, as Jesus came not just for the world but for you, for me, and for every heart willing to receive Him. The promise of the Savior is the reason we can have peace in troubled times, for we know that God is with us and that His love endures forever. His promise was not shaken by time or circumstances, and it is a reminder that God's word is true, steadfast, and eternal. He is the "God, that cannot lie," who "promised before the world began" (Titus 1:2).

This promise of the Savior brings us to a place of adoration. How can we not adore the One who came to save us, the One who loved us so much that He gave Himself completely for us? When we come to the manger, we see not just a baby but the fulfillment of God's unbreakable promise, a promise that cost Him everything. Christmas is an invitation to stand in awe of God's faithfulness and to adore Him with all our hearts. When we sing, "O come, let us adore Him," we are responding to a love that sought us, a love that rescued us, and a love that will never let us go. The promise of the Savior is a promise of eternal life, and through Jesus, we have the assurance that nothing can separate us from His love. "For I am persuaded, that neither death, nor life, nor angels, nor principalities, nor powers, nor things present, nor things to come, nor height, nor depth, nor any other creature, shall be able to separate us from the love of God, which is in Christ Jesus our Lord" (Romans 8:38-39).

In this promise, we find our hope, our peace, and our joy. As we reflect on this first chapter, let our hearts be filled with gratitude for the Savior who came to us, who fulfilled every word spoken about Him, and who invites us to live in the light of His love. His promise is our anchor, our assurance, and our song of praise. So, let us come and adore Him, the One who keeps His promises, who brings us salvation, and who, in every season, is faithful and true.

# Chapter 2 - Prophecy of Promised Peace

In "O Come, Let Us Adore Him: A Christmas Devotional," we come to marvel at the beauty and wonder of prophecy fulfilled in the birth of Jesus, a testament to God's faithfulness and unchanging love. Through the ages, the people of God waited with eager hearts for the promised Messiah, the one who would bring light to their darkness and salvation to their souls. Every page of the Old Testament, every promise spoken by prophets, pointed to the coming of a Savior, who would be born to redeem and restore what had been lost. The words of Isaiah echo through the centuries, reminding us of God's promise, "For unto us a child is born, unto us a son is given: and the government shall be upon his shoulder: and his name shall be called Wonderful, Counsellor, The mighty God, The everlasting Father, The Prince of Peace" (Isaiah 9:6). This prophecy was not just a hope; it was a certainty that God would fulfill His word at the perfect time. Jesus was born in Bethlehem, exactly as foretold, proving that God is faithful, that His promises are true, and that His love endures forever.

The fulfillment of prophecy in Jesus' birth stands as a reminder that God's plans are always on time and never fail. God spoke through His prophets, preparing the hearts of His people to recognize the Messiah when He came. Through Micah, God declared, "But thou, Bethlehem Ephratah, though thou be little among the thousands of Judah, yet out of thee shall he come forth unto me that is to be ruler in Israel" (Micah 5:2). In a small, unassuming town, the Savior was born, just as God had said. This shows us that even in our own lives, God's promises, no matter how improbable they may seem, will come to pass. Jesus' birth reminds us that God keeps His word, that He is both sovereign and close, working in ways we may not always understand but can fully trust.

The prophecy fulfilled in Christ's birth is a testament to God's faithfulness across generations. He spoke through prophets like Isaiah, Jeremiah, and

Micah, who foretold not only the coming of the Savior but also the love and compassion that would accompany Him. As Jeremiah wrote, "Behold, the days come, saith the Lord, that I will raise unto David a righteous Branch, and a King shall reign and prosper" (Jeremiah 23:5). In Jesus, this prophecy was fulfilled, for He is the righteous Branch, the King who brings peace and salvation. He did not come with earthly splendor or worldly power but in humility, born in a stable, accessible to all who would seek Him. Every detail of Jesus' birth, from the lineage of David to the place of Bethlehem, fulfills prophecies spoken long before, showing that God's word stands firm and that His love for us is woven into every promise He makes.

As we reflect on the birth of Christ, we see the beauty of God's perfect plan unfolding before our eyes. "The LORD hath made bare his holy arm in the eyes of all the nations; and all the ends of the earth shall see the salvation of our God" (Isaiah 52:10). The coming of Jesus is the unveiling of God's salvation, a light to all people, a fulfillment of the ancient words that spoke of a day when joy and peace would come to earth. Jesus' birth was the dawning of this joy, the fulfillment of the hope that had been kindled in the hearts of believers through the centuries. In Christ, every prophecy about the Messiah found its fulfillment. His coming was not just an event but a divine act that continues to impact our lives today, assuring us that God's faithfulness is unwavering.

The prophecies about Jesus' birth remind us that God sees the bigger picture. He orchestrated history to prepare the world for the arrival of His Son, even when people could not see the full scope of His plan. When Isaiah prophesied, "Therefore the Lord himself shall give you a sign; Behold, a virgin shall conceive, and bear a son, and shall call his name Immanuel" (Isaiah 7:14), he spoke of a miraculous birth that would change the course of humanity. This sign of a virgin birth was fulfilled when Mary, a young woman chosen by God, brought forth the Savior of the world. This miracle reminds us that nothing is impossible with God and that His plans are higher than our understanding. Jesus' birth fulfilled prophecies that seemed beyond comprehension, yet they were fulfilled with perfect precision, affirming that God's promises are always certain.

Christ's birth was not only a fulfillment of prophecy but also an invitation for us to trust in God's faithfulness. Each prophecy that came to pass with the birth of Jesus is a reminder that God's word never returns void. He is the God who watches over His promises, who speaks and acts according to His loving purpose. "God is not a man, that he should lie; neither the son of man, that he should repent: hath he said, and shall he not do it?" (Numbers 23:19). As we celebrate Christmas, we are invited to look at the fulfilled prophecies and be encouraged in our own faith, knowing that the God who kept His promises then will keep His promises now.

The birth of Jesus fulfilled the ancient longing for a Savior, a hope that lay dormant for centuries but was awakened on that holy night in Bethlehem. Simeon, a devout man who waited for the "consolation of Israel," knew that the birth of Jesus was the fulfillment of God's promise. When he held the infant Christ in his arms, he proclaimed, "Lord, now lettest thou thy servant depart in peace, according to thy word: for mine eyes have seen thy salvation" (Luke 2:29-30). Simeon's words echo the fulfillment of prophecy and the peace that comes from knowing God's promises are true. In Jesus, we find this peace, a peace that fills our hearts as we trust in the One who fulfilled every word spoken about Him.

The fulfilled prophecies about Christ's birth are a reminder that God's timing is perfect. He orchestrated every detail, working across generations to bring about His purpose. The Apostle Paul echoes this truth, saying, "But when the fulness of the time was come, God sent forth his Son, made of a woman, made under the law" (Galatians 4:4). Jesus came at the exact moment God had planned, showing us that even in our waiting, God is working. His timing is never late, never early, but always right on time. As we look at the prophecies fulfilled in Jesus' birth, we are encouraged to trust God's timing in our own lives, knowing that His plans are for our good and His glory.

In the story of Jesus' birth, we see prophecy after prophecy fulfilled with absolute faithfulness. From His miraculous conception to His humble birth in Bethlehem, every detail was foretold and came to pass exactly as God had said. This gives us confidence in God's word, knowing that the same God who kept His promises then is the One who holds us now. "Forever, O Lord, thy word is settled in heaven" (Psalm 119:89). The birth of Christ is a celebration of God's unbreakable promises, a reminder that His word endures forever and that we can rely on Him completely.

As we celebrate the birth of Jesus, we are reminded that God's faithfulness never fails. He is the God who fulfills His word, who brings light into our darkness, and who remains with us always. This Christmas, as we reflect on the prophecy fulfilled in Christ, let our hearts be filled with gratitude for a God who keeps His promises. Let us come and adore the One who was promised, the One who has come to bring salvation, peace, and joy to the world.

# Chapter 3 - Prince of Peace

In "O Come, Let Us Adore Him: A Christmas Devotional," we reflect on the beautiful truth that Jesus, the Prince of Peace, came into a world filled with turmoil to bring a peace that calms even the greatest storms in our hearts. The prophecy in Isaiah 9:6 proclaimed, "For unto us a child is born, unto us a son is given: and the government shall be upon his shoulder: and his name shall be called Wonderful, Counsellor, The mighty God, The everlasting Father, The Prince of Peace." This title, Prince of Peace, speaks to His role as the one who brings stillness to every kind of chaos, whether it be the external pressures of life or the inner battles that rage within. Jesus Himself assured us of this peace, saying, "Peace I leave with you, my peace I give unto you: not as the world giveth, give I unto you. Let not your heart be troubled, neither let it be afraid" (John 14:27). His peace is unlike anything the world can offer; it is enduring, calming, and rooted in His eternal love.

As the Prince of Peace, Jesus is the answer to the unrest that fills our hearts. When we are weighed down by fears, anxieties, and uncertainties, He invites us to find rest in Him. He promised, "Come unto me, all ye that labour and are heavy laden, and I will give you rest" (Matthew 11:28). This rest is not simply a pause from troubles but a deep, abiding peace that comes from knowing we are held by a God who loves us completely. This peace was God's gift to us through the birth of Jesus, a gift that brings calm to every storm and assurance to every worry. Even when the world around us seems chaotic, His peace guards our hearts and minds. As Philippians 4:7 reminds us, "And the peace of God, which passeth all understanding, shall keep your hearts and minds through Christ Jesus." This peace is beyond our comprehension, but it is the steadying force that holds us when everything else feels unstable.

The Prince of Peace doesn't promise a life free from challenges, but He promises His presence with us in every trial. He is with us in every valley, in every dark night, bringing His light and comfort. David understood this when he wrote, "Yea, though I walk through the valley of the shadow of death, I will fear no evil: for thou art with me; thy rod and thy staff they comfort me" (Psalm 23:4). Jesus, our Prince of Peace, walks with us through every difficulty, surrounding us with His love and protection, calming our fears with His presence. He is the shepherd who cares for His sheep, leading us beside still waters and restoring our souls.

The peace that Jesus brings also reconciles us to God. Through His sacrifice, He bridged the gap between us and our Creator, offering us forgiveness and a new relationship with the Father. As Romans 5:1 declares, "Therefore being justified by faith, we have peace with God through our Lord Jesus Christ." This peace with God is the foundation of all other peace, for when our hearts are right with God, we find true rest for our souls. The Prince of Peace came to remove the barriers of sin and to restore us to a relationship with God, giving us a lasting peace that nothing can take away. His death and resurrection assure us that we are no longer separated from God, but are welcomed into His family as His beloved children.

Jesus, the Prince of Peace, also brings peace into our relationships with others. He teaches us to forgive, to love, and to be peacemakers in a world that often chooses conflict. He said, "Blessed are the peacemakers: for they shall be called the children of God" (Matthew 5:9). As followers of the Prince of Peace, we are called to reflect His love and compassion, to be instruments of peace wherever we go. When we let His peace fill our hearts, it overflows into our interactions with others, softening our words, calming our reactions, and helping us to live in harmony. Jesus empowers us to let go of anger, to seek reconciliation, and to love our neighbors as ourselves.

In moments of fear and anxiety, Jesus stands as our Prince of Peace, whispering calm to our troubled hearts. He reminds us of His presence and invites us to trust in His goodness. "Fear thou not; for I am with thee: be not dismayed; for I am thy God: I will strengthen thee; yea, I will help thee; yea, I will uphold thee with the right hand of my righteousness" (Isaiah 41:10). This peace is anchored in His promises and in the certainty of His unchanging nature. The world may change, and circumstances may shift, but His peace remains steady and secure. We can cast all our anxieties upon Him, knowing that He cares deeply for us. "Casting all your care upon him; for he careth for you" (1 Peter 5:7). His peace is not conditional on circumstances but is rooted in His constant presence and His love that never fails.

The Prince of Peace fills our hearts with joy even in trials, for His peace brings a hope that transcends difficulties. Paul reminds us of this when he says, "Now the God of hope fill you with all joy and peace in believing, that ye may abound in hope, through the power of the Holy Ghost" (Romans 15:13). This joy and peace are the evidence of His Spirit within us, reminding us that we belong to Him and that our future is secure in His hands. No matter what we face, we can rejoice, for the Prince of Peace is with us, guiding us through every storm and bringing us safely to His eternal rest.

As we come to adore the Prince of Peace, we find that His peace transforms us. It changes our outlook, fills us with hope, and strengthens our faith. He invites us to lay down our burdens, to let go of our fears, and to rest in His love. "Thou wilt keep him in perfect peace, whose mind is stayed on thee: because he trusteth in thee" (Isaiah 26:3). This perfect peace is available to us when we fix our eyes on Jesus, trusting in His faithfulness and goodness. In a world that often feels overwhelming, His peace is the anchor that holds us firm. As we reflect on this season of Christmas, let us remember that the Prince of Peace came to bring a peace that endures, a peace that fills our hearts with joy and hope, a peace that is our strength and comfort.

The Prince of Peace came for us, offering a peace that the world cannot give, a peace that will never fade. He is our calm in the storm, our shelter in times of trouble, and our assurance of God's love. This Christmas, may we come to Him with open hearts, ready to receive His peace and to let that peace transform our lives. For in Jesus, the Prince of Peace, we find everything we need: a love that comforts, a hope that sustains, and a peace that never ends.

# Chapter 4 - Perfect Providence in God's Plan

In "O Come, Let Us Adore Him: A Christmas Devotional," we are invited to marvel at God's perfect timing in sending His Son, Jesus Christ, into the world at the precise moment that had been ordained from the beginning. The Bible tells us, "But when the fulness of the time was come, God sent forth his Son" (Galatians 4:4). This phrase, "the fulness of time," speaks to God's divine providence, showing that every detail was orchestrated by His hand. When Jesus was born, it wasn't by chance or coincidence; it was the fulfillment of a divine plan, demonstrating that God is never late, nor is He early. His timing is always perfect. God's wisdom and providence shaped every moment, and each prophecy, each preparation, and each event unfolded exactly as He intended. God's timing is flawless, and this is a reminder that He is in control, not just of the big events in history, but of every detail in our lives as well. In moments when we feel like things aren't happening according to our plans, we can rest in the truth that God's timing is always right, and His plans are far greater than we could imagine. The arrival of Jesus on that holy night in Bethlehem was a testimony to God's faithfulness and His profound love for humanity.

God had been preparing for this moment from the very beginning. The Old Testament is filled with prophecies pointing to the coming of the Messiah, each one a glimpse into the promise that God would fulfill at just the right time. Through the prophets, God declared, "Therefore the Lord himself shall give you a sign; Behold, a virgin shall conceive, and bear a son, and shall call his name Immanuel" (Isaiah 7:14). Even when the people waited for generations, seemingly in silence, God's plan was unfolding, building toward this perfect moment. "For the vision is yet for an appointed time... though it tarry, wait for it; because it will surely come, it will not tarry" (Habakkuk 2:3). This tells us that God's promises will always come to pass, though sometimes it feels like we are waiting longer than we want. Jesus' birth reminds us that God is faithful, that He hears the cries of His people, and that He fulfills His word exactly as He said He would.

The timing of Jesus' birth was a demonstration of God's wisdom in setting everything in place. "Known unto God are all his works from the beginning of the world" (Acts 15:18). He chose the perfect era in history, a time when the Roman Empire had established roads and a common language that would allow the message of Jesus to spread throughout the world. Even the census that brought Mary and Joseph to Bethlehem was part of God's plan, ensuring that Jesus would be born in the very town prophesied by Micah: "But thou, Bethlehem Ephratah, though thou be little among the thousands of Judah, yet out of thee shall he come forth unto me that is to be ruler in Israel" (Micah 5:2). Every detail, every event leading up to the birth of Christ, was under God's control. He used emperors and rulers, shepherds and wise men, to bring His purpose to completion. This reminds us that no situation, no ruler, and no power is beyond God's sovereign control. In our lives, too, God is always working, even in ways we may not immediately see.

Jesus came not only in the right time in history but also at the right time for humanity's need. In a world longing for hope, for redemption, and for a Savior, Jesus came as the answer. Paul wrote, "For when we were yet without strength, in due time Christ died for the ungodly" (Romans 5:6). Jesus came when we were helpless, unable to save ourselves, and His arrival changed everything. Just as God knew the perfect time to send His Son, He knows the perfect time to act in our lives. When we feel weak, when we feel like we're in darkness, God's timing shines through, showing us that He has not abandoned us. We can trust in His perfect providence, knowing that He will always act in our best interest.

God's timing in sending Jesus is a reminder that He is intimately involved in the details of our lives. He sees our needs, our struggles, and our longings, and He acts at just the right time. "To every thing there is a season, and a time to every purpose under the heaven" (Ecclesiastes 3:1). Just as He brought Jesus into the world at the exact right moment, He knows the perfect timing for everything in our lives. When we're tempted to rush ahead or question why things aren't happening as quickly as we'd like, we can look to the birth of Christ as a reminder that God's timing is perfect and that He is always working things out according to His purpose.

In those times of waiting, God's timing teaches us patience and trust. We may not always understand why we are waiting, but we can be assured that God is not idle. "Wait on the Lord: be of good courage, and he shall strengthen thine heart" (Psalm 27:14). Waiting on God's timing is a test of our faith, but it is also an opportunity to grow in our relationship with Him, to learn to rely on His strength and wisdom rather than our own. Just as the people of Israel waited for the Messiah, we wait on God's promises with the assurance that He will fulfill them in His perfect time. Jesus' birth is the ultimate evidence of God's faithfulness, a sign that He will never leave us or forsake us.

As we reflect on the story of Christmas, let us remember that God's timing is always perfect. The same God who planned the birth of Christ, down to the smallest detail, is in control of our lives. He knows the desires of our hearts, He understands our fears, and He promises to guide us in His time. "Trust in the Lord with all thine heart; and lean not unto thine own understanding. In all thy ways acknowledge him, and he shall direct thy paths" (Proverbs 3:5-6). God's timing is an invitation to trust Him fully, to surrender our plans, and to believe that His ways are higher than ours. Just as He brought Jesus into the world at the perfect time, He will bring about His purpose in our lives.

The birth of Jesus at just the right time reminds us that God's timing is perfect, not just for the grand events of history, but for each moment of our lives. He sees the end from the beginning, and He knows what is best for us. "For I know the thoughts that I think toward you, saith the Lord, thoughts of peace, and not of evil, to give you an expected end" (Jeremiah 29:11). His timing is part of His love for us, a reflection of His desire to bring good into our lives. When we feel like things aren't happening as quickly as we would like, we can find peace in knowing that God's timing is always right.

The story of Christmas is a story of God's providence, a story that tells us we are not forgotten. Just as He fulfilled every prophecy, He will fulfill His promises to us. Jesus' birth is a reminder that God is faithful, that His timing is perfect, and that we are always held in His hands. As we celebrate Christmas, let us rest in the assurance that God's timing is perfect, that He sees us, and that He is working all things together for our good.

# Chapter 5 - Path of Profound Humility

In "O Come, Let Us Adore Him: A Christmas Devotional," we come to reflect on the remarkable humility of Christ, born in a simple manger, wrapped in swaddling clothes, and laid in a lowly place, showing us the beauty and power of humility. The King of Kings and Lord of Lords, who holds all power and authority, chose to enter our world not in a grand palace, but in a stable, surrounded by animals and the humblest of beginnings. "And she brought forth her firstborn son, and wrapped him in swaddling clothes, and laid him in a manger; because there was no room for them in the inn" (Luke 2:7). In His humility, Jesus showed us that true greatness is found in simplicity and love, not in power or wealth. He, who was in the form of God, took on the form of a servant, reminding us that humility is not a sign of weakness but of incredible strength and purpose. The apostle Paul captures this perfectly when he writes, "Let this mind be in you, which was also in Christ Jesus: Who, being in the form of God, thought it not robbery to be equal with God: But made himself of no reputation, and took upon him the form of a servant, and was made in the likeness of men" (Philippians 2:5-7). Jesus' birth in a humble setting reveals that God values the heart above all else, and His entrance into the world speaks to the humility that He embodied every day of His life.

The humility of Christ is a powerful reminder that God meets us in our lowest places. He is not distant or unreachable; He is Emmanuel, God with us, willing to come down into our world, into our struggles, and meet us exactly where we are. His birth in a manger was a deliberate act of humility, a choice to step away from the glory of heaven to be close to us. As Isaiah prophesied, "For thus saith the high and lofty One that inhabiteth eternity, whose name is Holy; I dwell in the high and holy place, with him also that is of a contrite and humble spirit" (Isaiah 57:15). Jesus' humble birth is a testament to God's love for the lowly, the broken, and the humble in heart. He chose a path of humility to show us that His kingdom is not about power as the world sees it but about service, love, and gentleness. Jesus said, "Take my yoke upon you, and learn of me; for I am meek and lowly in heart: and ye shall find rest unto your souls" (Matthew 11:29). His humility invites us to find rest in Him, to set aside pride, and to walk in gentleness and love.

Christ's humility is an example for us to follow. He showed us that life is not about exalting ourselves but about lifting others. Jesus said, "Whosoever shall exalt himself shall be abased; and he that shall humble himself shall be exalted" (Matthew 23:12). This is the paradox of God's kingdom: those who seek to elevate themselves will be brought low, but those who humble themselves will be lifted up. In Jesus' life and ministry, we see this truth lived out perfectly. He washed His disciples' feet, He healed the sick, He comforted the outcasts, and He laid down His life for us. Every action, every word, showed us what true humility looks like. He chose humility not out of necessity but out of love, showing us that in serving others, we fulfill the very heart of God. His life calls us to walk in humility, to serve without seeking recognition, and to love without expecting anything in return.

Jesus' birth in a stable teaches us that humility is not about what we lack, but about what we willingly give up for others. He gave up the glory of heaven to be with us, to experience life as we do, and to show us the depth of God's love. "For ye know the grace of our Lord Jesus Christ, that, though he was rich, yet for your sakes he became poor, that ye through his poverty might be rich" (2 Corinthians 8:9). He became poor so that we could know the riches of God's love, choosing a life of humility to bring us into a relationship with Him. In His humility, Jesus opened the way for us to come close to God, not through pride or self-righteousness, but through a humble heart that recognizes its need for Him. The manger in Bethlehem stands as a symbol of this humility, a place where the glory of God was revealed in the most unexpected way.

The humility of Christ is also a source of encouragement for us. He knows our struggles, our weaknesses, and our fears because He experienced them Himself. He came not as a distant ruler but as one who understands our humanity fully. "For we have not an high priest which cannot be touched with the feeling of our infirmities; but was in all points tempted like as we are, yet without sin" (Hebrews 4:15). Jesus' humble birth reminds us that He is not only our Savior but our Friend, one who walks with us in our joys and our sorrows. He invites us to bring our burdens to Him, to cast our cares on Him, for He cares deeply for us. In His humility, we find the love and compassion of a Savior who is always near, always present, and always willing to help us.

The humility of Christ also calls us to reflect on our own lives. Just as He humbled Himself, He invites us to live humbly, to seek God's approval above the approval of others, and to serve with a heart of love. "Humble yourselves therefore under the mighty hand of God, that he may exalt you in due time" (1 Peter 5:6). Humility is not a burden but a blessing, a way to align our hearts with God's heart, to find joy in serving others, and to discover the peace that comes from surrendering our will to His. Jesus' life shows us that true greatness is found not in power or status but in humility, in loving others, and in living a life that reflects God's love.

As we celebrate Christmas, let us remember the humility of Christ, who came into the world in the most humble of ways, showing us that God's love is not reserved for the powerful but is poured out for all, especially the humble and the lowly. His birth in a manger speaks volumes about the character of God, a God who values the heart over appearances, who draws near to those who are often overlooked, and who lifts up the lowly. "The Lord lifteth up the meek: he casteth the wicked down to the ground" (Psalm 147:6). His love for us is so great that He was willing to come as a child, to walk among us, and to lay down His life for us.

In the humility of Christ, we see the beauty of a Savior who did not come to be served, but to serve, and to give His life as a ransom for many. Let us come and adore Him, the humble King, who chose a manger over a throne, a life of service over a life of ease, and the cross over the comfort of heaven. His humility is an invitation for us to follow in His footsteps, to love as He loved, to serve as He served, and to live with a heart of humility that reflects His. This Christmas, may we be inspired by the humility of Christ, finding joy in the simple, peace in the humble, and love in serving others, just as He has loved and served us.

# Chapter 6 – Purity of the Promised Plan

In "O Come, Let Us Adore Him: A Christmas Devotional," we stand in awe of the miraculous and holy event that is the Virgin Birth, a mystery that displays the purity, power, and divine nature of God's plan. The angel's message to Mary reveals the sacredness of this moment: "Behold, a virgin shall be with child, and shall bring forth a son, and they shall call his name Emmanuel, which being interpreted is, God with us" (Matthew 1:23). This miraculous birth shows that God was breaking into history in a way that was beyond human understanding, setting apart the birth of Jesus as a divine act, untouched by sin or human will. The purity of the Virgin Birth speaks to the holiness of Jesus, who would be called "the Holy One of God" (Mark 1:24). Through this miraculous event, God showed that He is not limited by natural laws; rather, He is the Creator of all things and can work wonders beyond human ability. The birth of Jesus through a virgin was the fulfillment of prophecy and the beginning of a new chapter in God's story of redemption.

Mary, a humble and faithful young woman, received this news with wonder and reverence. She responded to the angel, saying, "Behold the handmaid of the Lord; be it unto me according to thy word" (Luke 1:38). In her humble acceptance, Mary became a vessel for God's miraculous plan, carrying the Savior of the world in purity and obedience. The Virgin Birth was not just a sign of God's power but also a reflection of His grace and purity. Jesus, conceived by the Holy Spirit, entered the world without the stain of sin, setting Him apart as the spotless Lamb of God who would take away the sins of the world. "For such an high priest became us, who is holy, harmless, undefiled, separate from sinners, and made higher than the heavens" (Hebrews 7:26). The purity of His birth speaks to the purity of His life, a life that was completely surrendered to the will of the Father.

Through the Virgin Birth, God demonstrated that His ways are higher than our ways, and His thoughts are higher than our thoughts. "For with God nothing shall be impossible" (Luke 1:37). What seemed impossible to human minds was accomplished by God's power, reminding us that there is nothing He cannot do. The birth of Jesus through a virgin is a testimony to His sovereignty and His ability to bring forth life in ways beyond our comprehension. This miracle stands as a reminder that God is always working, even in ways that may seem mysterious or impossible to us. It encourages us to trust in His promises and to believe that He is able to do exceedingly abundantly above all that we ask or think.

The Virgin Birth also speaks to the love of God, who chose to come close to us in the most humble and gentle way. He could have come in power and majesty, yet He chose to enter the world as a baby, born to a young woman in a small town. This choice reflects God's desire to be near to us, to be "Emmanuel, God with us" (Matthew 1:23). Jesus' birth in such a pure and humble way shows that God values the lowly and the humble. "For thus saith the high and lofty One that inhabiteth eternity, whose name is Holy; I dwell in the high and holy place, with him also that is of a contrite and humble spirit" (Isaiah 57:15). The birth of Jesus through a virgin was a holy event, designed by God to bring salvation to all who would believe, showing that He is not distant but near to those who seek Him in faith and humility.

The purity of the Virgin Birth is a call for us to seek purity in our own lives. Jesus, born without sin, lived a life that was holy and pleasing to God. He invites us to follow in His footsteps, to walk in holiness and humility, and to seek a heart that is pure before Him. "Blessed are the pure in heart: for they shall see God" (Matthew 5:8). The birth of Jesus is not only a celebration of God's miraculous power but also an invitation to live in a way that honors Him, striving for purity and surrender in all that we do. The Virgin Birth is a reminder that God desires hearts that are pure and open to His presence, just as Mary was when she said, "Be it unto me according to thy word."

As we reflect on the Virgin Birth, we are reminded of the beauty of God's grace and the depth of His love. He chose to enter our world in the purest way possible, through a young virgin who was willing to trust in His plan. This act of love shows us that God's ways are pure, His love is holy, and His grace is boundless. Jesus' birth is a symbol of God's willingness to reach down into our brokenness and bring us back to Himself. "For God so loved the world, that he gave his only begotten Son, that whosoever believeth in him should not perish, but have everlasting life" (John 3:16). The Virgin Birth is a sign of that love, a love that was willing to take on human form, to walk among us, and to bring us hope and salvation.

The Virgin Birth also fulfilled the ancient prophecies, showing that God's word is true and His promises are sure. "Therefore the Lord himself shall give you a sign; Behold, a virgin shall conceive, and bear a son, and shall call his name Immanuel" (Isaiah 7:14). This prophecy, spoken hundreds of years before Jesus' birth, was fulfilled in the birth of Christ, proving that God is faithful to His word. When we look at the Virgin Birth, we see a God who keeps His promises, who never fails to bring His word to pass. This gives us confidence in all of God's promises, reminding us that He is faithful and that we can trust Him completely.

The miracle of the Virgin Birth is also a reminder that God is the source of all life. He is the Creator who formed us in our mother's womb, and He is the One who brought forth life through Mary. "For thou hast possessed my reins: thou hast covered me in my mother's womb" (Psalm 139:13). The birth of Jesus through a virgin shows us that life is a gift from God, a sacred and holy gift that He alone can give. As we reflect on the birth of Christ, we are reminded of the miracle of life and the beauty of God's creation. The Virgin Birth speaks to the holiness of life and the power of God to bring forth life in miraculous ways.

The purity of the Virgin Birth is a call to worship and adore Jesus, the holy Son of God, who came to save us. "Worship the Lord in the beauty of holiness" (Psalm 29:2). This Christmas season, as we think about the birth of Jesus, let us come with hearts full of reverence and awe, marveling at the purity and holiness of this miraculous birth. Let us adore Him, the One who was born of a virgin, the One who came to bring light into our darkness, and the One who is worthy of all our praise and worship.

In the Virgin Birth, we see the perfect blend of God's power and humility, His majesty and His tenderness. Jesus, born of a virgin, came in purity to bring us salvation, to give us hope, and to invite us into a relationship with God. This miracle reminds us that God is always at work, even in ways that may seem mysterious or beyond our understanding. His plans are perfect, His love is pure, and His grace is enough for every need. This Christmas, as we celebrate the birth of Jesus, let us remember the purity and power of the Virgin Birth, and let our hearts be filled with gratitude for the love that God has shown us in Christ.

# Chapter 7 - Proclamation of Promised Peace

In "O Come, Let Us Adore Him: A Christmas Devotional," we celebrate the powerful moment when angels announced the birth of Christ to a world that was waiting, a world longing for hope and peace. The appearance of the angel to the shepherds in the quiet fields near Bethlehem was a proclamation of joy, one that echoed the love and promise of God across the heavens and into the hearts of all who would hear. "And, lo, the angel of the Lord came upon them, and the glory of the Lord shone round about them: and they were sore afraid" (Luke 2:9). The radiance of God's glory filled the night, and the fear the shepherds first felt quickly turned into awe as they heard the joyful message. The angel said to them, "Fear not: for, behold, I bring you good tidings of great joy, which shall be to all people" (Luke 2:10). This message was not only for kings or those in high places but was given to humble shepherds, showing that the Savior had come for everyone, regardless of status or position. The announcement was one of inclusivity, inviting all people to come and receive the good news of salvation and peace. This divine proclamation by the angels is a reminder that God's love is for everyone, that His peace is available to all who seek Him.

The angel's message declared the long-awaited arrival of the Messiah, saying, "For unto you is born this day in the city of David a Saviour, which is Christ the Lord" (Luke 2:11). This announcement confirmed that Jesus was the fulfillment of God's promises, the answer to the prayers of generations who had awaited the coming of the Savior. It was a moment when heaven met earth, and the joy of the angels filled the skies, proclaiming the greatness of God's love and His desire to be with His people. The angels, who had seen the face of God and understood His glory, could not contain their praise at the wonder of what God had done. "And suddenly there was with the angel a multitude of the heavenly host praising God, and saying, Glory to God in the highest, and on earth peace, good will toward men" (Luke 2:13-14). This chorus of praise was a heavenly song of peace, declaring that through Jesus, peace and goodwill were now offered to all humanity. This message of peace is one that resonates across time, offering comfort and hope to all who hear it, reminding us that God's desire is for peace in our hearts and in our lives.

The angels' announcement is also a call to joy. They brought "good tidings of great joy" (Luke 2:10), a joy that was meant to fill the hearts of all people. This joy is not fleeting or dependent on circumstances but is rooted in the eternal truth that God has come to be with us. This joy is the light that shines in the darkness, the assurance that we are not alone, and the promise that God's love is greater than any fear or sorrow. The shepherds, upon hearing this message, were filled with wonder and awe. They left their flocks to go and see the Savior, and their lives were forever changed. "And it came to pass, as the angels were gone away from them into heaven, the shepherds said one to another, Let us now go even unto Bethlehem, and see this thing which is come to pass, which the Lord hath made known unto us" (Luke 2:15). Their response to the angelic message was one of faith and eagerness, a willingness to seek the Savior and to experience the truth of the proclamation for themselves.

The angelic proclamation is a reminder to us of the beauty and importance of sharing the good news of Christ's birth. Just as the angels could not keep silent but had to declare the glory of God and the joy of the Savior's arrival, we too are called to share the message of Jesus with those around us. "Go ye into all the world, and preach the gospel to every creature" (Mark 16:15). The angels' proclamation encourages us to spread the message of God's love, peace, and joy, to be bearers of light in a world that needs hope. The good news of Jesus is a message for all people, and like the angels, we are invited to proclaim it boldly and joyfully. The angels remind us that this message is not only for our own hearts but is meant to be shared, to reach the hearts of others, and to bring joy to all who will receive it.

The angels' message also speaks of peace, a peace that only Jesus can bring. They declared, "Glory to God in the highest, and on earth peace, good will toward men" (Luke 2:14). This peace is not simply the absence of conflict but is a deep and abiding peace that comes from knowing God and being in relationship with Him. Jesus, the Prince of Peace, came to bring reconciliation between God and humanity, offering a peace that transcends all understanding.

"And the peace of God, which passeth all understanding, shall keep your hearts and minds through Christ Jesus" (Philippians 4:7). This peace is a gift that God offers to each of us, a peace that fills our hearts and calms our fears. The angels' proclamation invites us to receive this peace and to let it guide our lives, reminding us that in Christ, we have a peace that the world cannot give.

The proclamation of the angels is also a testament to the faithfulness of God. The birth of Jesus was the fulfillment of ancient prophecies, promises that God had made to His people long ago. Through the prophets, God had declared that a Savior would come, and the angels' message confirmed that God had kept His word. "Therefore the Lord himself shall give you a sign; Behold, a virgin shall conceive, and bear a son, and shall call his name Immanuel" (Isaiah 7:14). The angels' announcement reminds us that God is faithful, that His promises are true, and that He fulfills His word in His perfect timing. This assurance of God's faithfulness gives us hope, reminding us that just as He kept His promises then, He will keep His promises to us today.

The shepherds, upon hearing the proclamation of the angels, did not hesitate to seek the Savior. Their hearts were moved by the message, and they responded with faith and action. "And they came with haste, and found Mary, and Joseph, and the babe lying in a manger" (Luke 2:16). The shepherds' response is a beautiful example of faith, showing us that when we hear the good news of Jesus, we are invited to come and see, to draw near to Him, and to experience the truth of His love for ourselves. The angels' message is not only a call to believe but also a call to seek, to come close to Jesus, and to find in Him the hope and peace that we need.

The angels' proclamation continues to resonate today, reminding us that the joy of Christmas is not just for a single night but is a joy that is meant to fill our lives every day. The good news of Jesus' birth is a message that brings hope, peace, and joy to all who hear it. This Christmas season, as we remember the angels' announcement, let us open our hearts to the wonder and beauty of this divine proclamation. Let us come and adore Him, the Savior who has come to bring us peace, the Lord who has come to bring us joy, and the King who is worthy of all our praise. The angels' message is a reminder that God's love is for everyone, that His peace is available to all, and that His joy is ours to receive. As we celebrate Christmas, may we carry the angels' proclamation in our hearts, sharing the good news of Jesus with those around us, and rejoicing in the gift of salvation that He has brought to us all.

# Chapter 8 – Promise of Profound Joy

In "O Come, Let Us Adore Him: A Christmas Devotional," we are reminded of the profound joy and hope that came to the world through the birth of Jesus Christ, a moment when the angels proclaimed "good tidings of great joy, which shall be to all people" (Luke 2:10). This announcement is not just a historical event; it is an everlasting message of joy and hope meant for every heart that hears it. The angel's words, spoken to humble shepherds in the quiet fields near Bethlehem, carried a divine proclamation that continues to resound through the ages. Jesus' birth was the fulfillment of promises made long ago, a sign that God had not forgotten His people and that salvation had come. This good news is for everyone, reminding us that God's love is boundless, and His grace is extended to all who would believe. The arrival of Christ in the world is the ultimate source of joy, a joy that lifts burdens, dispels fears, and fills hearts with peace. This joy is unlike anything the world can give; it is a joy that comes from knowing that God is with us, that He has come to be our Savior, and that His love is unchanging.

The good news of Christ's birth brings joy to our lives because it speaks to our deepest needs. Jesus came to bring light to those who walk in darkness, to lift up the brokenhearted, and to offer peace to those who are weary and burdened. "The Spirit of the Lord is upon me, because he hath anointed me to preach the gospel to the poor; he hath sent me to heal the brokenhearted, to preach deliverance to the captives, and recovering of sight to the blind, to set at liberty them that are bruised" (Luke 4:18). This mission, declared by Jesus, was God's answer to humanity's longing for hope and salvation. His birth was the beginning of God's plan to reconcile us to Himself, to bring peace to our hearts, and to show us the depth of His love. The joy of Christmas is rooted in the truth that we are loved, that we are not alone, and that God has made a way for us to be with Him forever.

The joy of Christ's birth is a joy that sustains us even in difficult times. Life may bring challenges, uncertainties, and sorrows, but the joy that comes from knowing Jesus is a joy that cannot be shaken. Jesus said, "These things have I spoken unto you, that my joy might remain in you, and that your joy might be full" (John 15:11). This joy is a gift from God, a joy that fills our hearts with peace and confidence, even when circumstances are tough. The good news of great joy is not dependent on the world around us but is grounded in the unchanging love of God. This joy is the light that shines in our darkness, the assurance that God is with us, and the promise that His love will never fail.

The announcement of Jesus' birth was a declaration of God's goodness, a message of love and hope sent from heaven to earth. "For unto you is born this day in the city of David a Saviour, which is Christ the Lord" (Luke 2:11). This message, given first to the shepherds, was a message for all people, a proclamation that the Savior had come. The shepherds, upon hearing this good news, were filled with joy and wonder. They hurried to Bethlehem to see the baby, and their lives were forever changed. "And they came with haste, and found Mary, and Joseph, and the babe lying in a manger" (Luke 2:16). Their response to the good news is a reminder to us of the joy and eagerness that should fill our hearts as we come to Jesus, as we recognize that in Him, we find all that we need.

The good news of great joy is a reminder that God's love is for everyone. This message was not delivered to kings or rulers but to shepherds, showing that God's love is not limited by status or position. "The Lord is nigh unto them that are of a broken heart; and saveth such as be of a contrite spirit" (Psalm 34:18). Jesus came for the humble, the lowly, and the weary, offering hope to all who would receive Him. His birth is a testament to God's inclusive love, a love that reaches every corner of the earth, inviting all people to come and find joy in Him. This joy is not just for a select few; it is for all who will believe, for all who will open their hearts to the Savior.

This good news of great joy is also a call to share this joy with others. Just as the angels could not contain their praise, we too are invited to spread the message of God's love, to proclaim the good news of Jesus to those around us. "Go ye into all the world, and preach the gospel to every creature" (Mark 16:15). The joy we have in Jesus is a joy meant to be shared, a light meant to shine in the lives of others. As we celebrate Christmas, let us remember that the good news of Christ's birth is a gift we are called to give to the world, a message of hope and peace that can transform hearts and bring joy to all who hear it.

The joy of Christ's birth is a joy that brings peace to our hearts. When we understand the depth of God's love for us, when we realize that He sent His Son to save us, we are filled with a peace that surpasses all understanding. "And the peace of God, which passeth all understanding, shall keep your hearts and minds through Christ Jesus" (Philippians 4:7). This peace is part of the great joy that comes from knowing Jesus, a peace that calms our fears and steadies our hearts. The good news of Christmas is a message of peace, a proclamation that through Jesus, we are reconciled to God, and we can live in the assurance of His love.

The birth of Jesus is good news of great joy because it shows us that God's promises are true. The prophets had foretold the coming of the Messiah, and in Jesus, every prophecy was fulfilled. "Therefore the Lord himself shall give you a sign; Behold, a virgin shall conceive, and bear a son, and shall call his name Immanuel" (Isaiah 7:14). The fulfillment of these promises is a reminder that God is faithful, that His word is sure, and that we can trust Him completely. The joy of Christmas is rooted in this truth, in the certainty that God is with us, that He is for us, and that He will never leave us.

The good news of Jesus' birth brings a joy that is eternal. This joy is not just for one season but is a joy that fills our hearts every day as we walk with Jesus. "Rejoice in the Lord alway: and again I say, Rejoice" (Philippians 4:4). The joy of knowing Jesus is a joy that sustains us, a joy that lifts us up, and a joy that reminds us of the hope we have in Him. This Christmas, as we reflect on the good news of Christ's birth, let our hearts be filled with this great joy, a joy that comes from knowing that we are loved, that we are saved, and that we have a Savior who is with us always.

The angels' message of good tidings is a reminder that Jesus came to bring joy to all people. This joy is a gift from God, a gift that fills our hearts with peace, love, and hope. As we celebrate Christmas, let us remember the joy of this good news, let us share it with others, and let us rejoice in the love of God that has come to us through Jesus Christ. This is the joy of Christmas, a joy that will never fade, a joy that is ours forever in Christ.

# Chapter 9 – Prelude to Divine Glory

In "O Come, Let Us Adore Him: A Christmas Devotional," we are inspired by the glorious song of the angels on that first Christmas night, proclaiming, "Glory to God in the highest, and on earth peace, good will toward men" (Luke 2:14). The angels' words remind us to give glory to God, not only in the joyful times but in every season, for He is worthy of our praise. The angels, who stood in the presence of God, knew His power, His majesty, and His love, and on that night, they could not keep silent. Heaven opened, and the angels sang for all to hear, glorifying the One who sent His Son to bring peace and redemption to a broken world. This heavenly praise echoes through time, inviting us to join in giving honor to the Lord, who is good, merciful, and full of grace. Their proclamation, "Glory to God in the highest," calls us to lift our voices, to exalt His name above all else, for He alone is worthy of such glory. This message is not just for Christmas; it is a timeless call to praise and honor the Creator who loved us so deeply that He sent His only Son to be our Savior.

The angels' song brings us back to the heart of worship, reminding us that our lives are meant to glorify God. "Give unto the Lord the glory due unto his name; worship the Lord in the beauty of holiness" (Psalm 29:2). When we recognize the greatness of God, our hearts naturally respond with praise. We see His hand in creation, His goodness in our lives, and His love displayed in the gift of Jesus. Every breath we take, every blessing we receive, and every moment we live is a reason to glorify Him. Like the angels, we are called to proclaim His glory, to let our lives be a testament to His love and faithfulness. The glory of God is not limited to a single event; it shines in every aspect of His creation, in the wonders of the earth and the heavens, and in the lives of those who have experienced His saving grace. "The heavens declare the glory of God; and the firmament sheweth his handywork" (Psalm 19:1). The angels' song is an invitation to join the heavenly chorus, to give our hearts to worship, and to glorify the One who is above all.

This call to give glory to God is a reminder that praise should be a part of our daily lives. "By him therefore let us offer the sacrifice of praise to God continually, that is, the fruit of our lips giving thanks to his name" (Hebrews 13:15). True praise comes from a heart that is filled with gratitude, recognizing that every good and perfect gift comes from Him. Even in challenging times, we are called to lift our voices in praise, knowing that God is with us, that He is working in our lives, and that His love never fails. The angels' proclamation of "Glory to God in the highest" is a call to us to remember His faithfulness, to trust in His goodness, and to honor Him with our lives. When we give glory to God, we find peace and joy, for praise connects us to the One who is the source of all comfort, hope, and love.

The angels' song also reminds us of the peace that comes from knowing God. Their proclamation was not only about giving glory to God but also about the peace He brings to those who trust in Him. "Thou wilt keep him in perfect peace, whose mind is stayed on thee: because he trusteth in thee" (Isaiah 26:3). This peace is a gift from God, a peace that surpasses all understanding and fills our hearts even in the midst of trials. Jesus, the Prince of Peace, came to bring reconciliation between God and humanity, offering us a peace that is rooted in His love and grace. The angels' message of peace is a reminder that God's love is constant, that His presence is with us, and that He desires for us to live in harmony with Him and with one another.

When we give glory to God, we align our hearts with His, and in doing so, we experience the peace that only He can give. "And the peace of God, which passeth all understanding, shall keep your hearts and minds through Christ Jesus" (Philippians 4:7). This peace is a byproduct of praise, a reminder that when we focus on God's goodness, His greatness, and His love, our fears and anxieties diminish, replaced by a sense of calm that only His presence can bring. The angels' message, "Glory to God in the highest, and on earth peace," speaks to the transformative power of praise, a power that brings tranquility to our souls and reminds us that we are held in the hands of a loving Father.

The angels' song of praise also reminds us that Jesus' birth was an act of God's love for all people. Their message was "good tidings of great joy, which shall be to all people" (Luke 2:10), a proclamation that God's love and salvation are available to everyone. This universal invitation to receive His love and to glorify Him transcends boundaries and brings people together in a shared hope. The glory of God is not exclusive; it is for all who would come to Him, for all who would seek His face and embrace His grace. In giving glory to God, we acknowledge His sovereignty, His kindness, and His open invitation for everyone to find life, hope, and salvation in Him.

The angels' praise on that holy night in Bethlehem is a reminder that God is worthy of glory in every season of our lives. "I will bless the Lord at all times: his praise shall continually be in my mouth" (Psalm 34:1). Whether we are in moments of joy or seasons of difficulty, God is with us, and He deserves our honor and praise. Just as the angels declared His glory with joy and reverence, we too are invited to praise Him in all circumstances, to lift our voices in thanksgiving, and to trust in His unfailing love. This act of giving glory to God is a powerful expression of faith, a declaration that we believe in His goodness, His strength, and His presence in our lives.

The angels' proclamation of "Glory to God in the highest" encourages us to live lives that reflect His glory. When we honor God with our words, our actions, and our hearts, we become a light in the world, a reflection of His love and grace. "Let your light so shine before men, that they may see your good works, and glorify your Father which is in heaven" (Matthew 5:16). Our lives are an opportunity to give glory to God, to show others the beauty of His love, and to invite them to experience the joy and peace that come from knowing Him. The angels' song calls us to live in a way that honors God, to let our lives be a testimony of His grace, and to bring glory to His name in all that we do.

As we celebrate Christmas, let us remember the angels' song and the call to give glory to God in the highest. Let us come before Him with hearts full of praise, recognizing that His love is endless, His mercy is boundless, and His grace is freely given to all who seek Him. Let us join the heavenly chorus, giving glory to the One who sent His Son to be our Savior, our Redeemer, and our Friend. This Christmas, may our hearts be filled with the same awe and reverence that filled the angels on that holy night, and may we give glory to God in all that we say and do.

# Chapter 10 – Pursuit of Divine Presence

In "O Come, Let Us Adore Him: A Christmas Devotional," we are drawn into the beautiful story of the shepherds who, with hearts full of faith and wonder, pursued the Savior upon hearing the angel's proclamation on that holy night. Out in the fields, watching over their flocks under the vast, star-filled sky, these shepherds were humble, quiet, and unassuming. Yet, in a moment, their lives were forever changed. Suddenly, an angel of the Lord appeared to them, and the glory of the Lord shone around, filling the night with a light and presence that they had never known before. "And, lo, the angel of the Lord came upon them, and the glory of the Lord shone round about them: and they were sore afraid" (Luke 2:9). Their fear quickly turned to awe as the angel spoke words that would resound through the ages, words of joy, hope, and fulfillment: "Fear not: for, behold, I bring you good tidings of great joy, which shall be to all people. For unto you is born this day in the city of David a Saviour, which is Christ the Lord" (Luke 2:10-11). In that moment, the shepherds were given a gift of divine revelation—a glimpse into the glorious plan of God to bring salvation to all people. Their hearts were stirred, filled with a longing to see this Savior, this newborn King who had come to bring peace on earth.

With eagerness and faith, they said to one another, "Let us now go even unto Bethlehem, and see this thing which is come to pass, which the Lord hath made known unto us" (Luke 2:15). Without hesitation, without delay, they left behind their flocks and set out in pursuit of Jesus, driven by an uncontainable desire to behold the Messiah. Their journey was not one of obligation or mere curiosity but one of joyful pursuit, born out of a deep belief in the message they had received. Their steps were guided by faith and a heart full of wonder, a desire to draw near to the very presence of God. The fields they left behind and the familiar paths they traveled were now infused with a holy purpose, as they sought the One who had been promised, the One who would bring light into a world filled with darkness. Their journey to Bethlehem is a testament to the power of faith and the beauty of a heart that is open to God's call.

When they arrived, the shepherds found exactly what the angel had promised. There, in a humble stable, lay Jesus, wrapped in swaddling clothes and lying in a manger. "And they came with haste, and found Mary, and Joseph, and the babe lying in a manger" (Luke 2:16). In that simple and quiet setting, they encountered the Savior, the very Son of God, in the most unassuming form—as a newborn child. Their eyes beheld the One who was foretold by the prophets, the One who would save His people from their sins. In that moment, all the promises, prophecies, and hopes of generations were fulfilled. The shepherds' pursuit of Jesus brought them face to face with the love of God, a love that had come down to dwell among us, to bring salvation to all who would believe. The scene before them was one of profound humility and holiness, a silent declaration of God's desire to be near to His people, to walk among them, and to offer them the gift of eternal life.

The shepherds' response to this miraculous encounter was not one of silence or restraint; their hearts overflowed with joy and praise. "And when they had seen it, they made known abroad the saying which was told them concerning this child" (Luke 2:17). They could not keep the news to themselves, for they had witnessed the greatest gift ever given, the birth of the Savior of the world. Their journey to find Jesus became a journey to share Him with others, to proclaim the good news of His coming to all who would listen. Their pursuit of Jesus transformed them from humble shepherds into the first messengers of the gospel, bearing witness to the light that had come into the world. The joy they experienced in that stable spilled over into their lives, compelling them to share the hope and love they had found. Their pursuit of Jesus became a lifelong testimony of God's grace, a proclamation of His goodness and mercy to all.

In the shepherds' response, we see a beautiful example of how we, too, are called to pursue Jesus with hearts full of faith and wonder. Their story is a reminder that God's invitation is extended to all, to the humble, the lowly, and the overlooked. Just as He revealed the birth of His Son to the shepherds, He calls each of us to draw near, to seek Him with a heart that is open and eager to know Him. "Seek ye the Lord while he may be found, call ye upon him while he is near" (Isaiah 55:6). The shepherds' pursuit of Jesus was marked by a joyful urgency, a willingness to leave behind their routine and comfort in order to experience the presence of God. In their response, we are encouraged to pursue Jesus with the same eagerness, to seek Him in every season of our lives, and to let our hearts be filled with the wonder of His love.

The shepherds' journey is a powerful reminder that faith is not passive; it is active, vibrant, and alive. Their response to the angel's message was one of immediate action, a decision to go and see, to pursue the truth of what they had been told. "But without faith it is impossible to please him: for he that cometh to God must believe that he is, and that he is a rewarder of them that diligently seek him" (Hebrews 11:6). Their faith was not based on what they could see but on the message they had received, a message that stirred their hearts and called them to action. In their pursuit of Jesus, we are reminded that true faith moves us, it compels us to seek God, to draw near to Him, and to experience the fullness of His love. Their journey to Bethlehem is a testimony of a faith that trusts, a faith that believes, and a faith that pursues God with all that we are.

As we reflect on the shepherds' response, we are invited to approach God with the same humility and openness. They did not question or doubt; they simply believed and responded. In their example, we see the beauty of a heart that is willing to receive God's message, a heart that is ready to embrace His love and follow His call. "The Lord is nigh unto them that are of a broken heart; and saveth such as be of a contrite spirit" (Psalm 34:18). The shepherds were ordinary people, yet they were chosen to be the first witnesses of the Savior's birth because of their humble and open hearts. Their story encourages us to approach God with humility, to come before Him with a heart that is willing to listen, and to respond with faith and wonder.

The shepherds' pursuit of Jesus is a call to us to seek God with all our hearts, to pursue Him with a passion that reflects our love and gratitude. They left behind their flocks, their livelihood, and their comfort to find the Savior, a reminder that following Jesus often requires us to leave behind what is familiar in order to experience the fullness of His presence. "Draw nigh to God, and he will draw nigh to you" (James 4:8). In their pursuit of Jesus, we are reminded that when we seek Him, we find Him, and in finding Him, we discover the joy, peace, and love that only He can give.

The shepherds' journey to Bethlehem was a journey of transformation, a journey that changed their lives forever. Their pursuit of Jesus led them to the heart of God, to the realization of His promises, and to the joy of His presence. This Christmas, as we reflect on their story, may we be inspired to pursue Jesus with all our hearts, to seek Him in every season of our lives, and to find in Him the fulfillment of every longing, the answer to every prayer, and the joy that never fades. Just as the shepherds went with haste, may we respond to God's call, may we come before Him with hearts of worship, and may we find in Him the peace, joy, and love that only He can give.

# Chapter 11 – Portrait of Persevering Faith

In "O Come, Let Us Adore Him: A Christmas Devotional," we are deeply moved by the story of Mary and her unwavering faith in God's plan, a faith that shines as a powerful example of trust and perseverance. Mary, a young woman from Nazareth, was chosen by God for a purpose beyond human understanding: to be the mother of His only Son, Jesus Christ. When the angel Gabriel appeared to her, bringing a message of extraordinary significance, she listened with a heart open to God's will. Gabriel declared, "Hail, thou that art highly favoured, the Lord is with thee: blessed art thou among women" (Luke 1:28). Despite her initial fear and confusion, Mary's faith was evident as she received this message with humility and courage. The angel continued, explaining that she would conceive and bear a son, and that His name would be Jesus, for He would be great and called the Son of the Highest. "And, behold, thou shalt conceive in thy womb, and bring forth a son, and shalt call his name JESUS" (Luke 1:31). Faced with an unimaginable calling, Mary could have been overwhelmed by doubt, but instead, she responded with words of pure faith: "Behold the handmaid of the Lord; be it unto me according to thy word" (Luke 1:38). Her obedience and willingness to accept God's plan, no matter the cost, show a perseverance rooted in trust and love for the Lord.

Mary's faith teaches us that true perseverance means trusting in God's promises even when the path ahead is uncertain. She accepted God's plan, knowing it would require courage and sacrifice. Mary understood that her calling would not be easy, as she would face doubt, judgment, and potential rejection from others, yet she remained steadfast. Her example reminds us that faith does not eliminate challenges but strengthens us to face them. "Trust in the Lord with all thine heart; and lean not unto thine own understanding" (Proverbs 3:5). Mary's willingness to surrender her life to God's will, despite the unknowns, is a testament to the power of a heart fully yielded to the Lord. She did not rely on her own understanding but trusted that God's plan was perfect, and she was willing to walk in obedience no matter what lay ahead.

As we reflect on Mary's journey, we see the beauty of a life lived in complete submission to God. Her response to Gabriel's message, "Behold the handmaid of the Lord," reveals her humble acceptance of her role in God's plan. She embraced her identity as a servant of the Lord, showing that true faith is not about seeking our own way but about surrendering to God's purposes. Mary's faith reminds us that God's plans are often beyond our comprehension, yet they are always good. "For I know the thoughts that I think toward you, saith the Lord, thoughts of peace, and not of evil, to give you an expected end" (Jeremiah 29:11). Mary's life is a testament to the peace and strength that come from trusting God's wisdom, knowing that He is working for our ultimate good.

Mary's perseverance in faith is also a reminder of God's faithfulness. As she carried Jesus, she carried the fulfillment of God's promises. From the beginning of time, God had promised a Savior, and through Mary's faith, that promise was brought to life. "Therefore the Lord himself shall give you a sign; Behold, a virgin shall conceive, and bear a son, and shall call his name Immanuel" (Isaiah 7:14). Mary's role in God's plan was a fulfillment of prophecy, a testimony to God's unwavering commitment to redeem His people. Her faith became a bridge between prophecy and fulfillment, showing us that God's promises never fail. In her perseverance, Mary bore witness to the truth that God's word is unchanging, and His love endures forever.

Mary's journey was not without trials. She faced questions, doubts, and fears, yet she remained committed to God's call. When she visited her cousin Elizabeth, who was also experiencing a miraculous pregnancy, Mary found encouragement and confirmation of God's work. Elizabeth, filled with the Holy Spirit, proclaimed, "Blessed art thou among women, and blessed is the fruit of thy womb. And whence is this to me, that the mother of my Lord should come to me?" (Luke 1:42-43). In this moment, Mary's faith was strengthened, as she saw that God was orchestrating every detail of His plan. The joy and affirmation she received from Elizabeth served as a reminder that God is faithful, even when the journey is difficult. Mary's perseverance teaches us to find strength in community, to seek encouragement from others who share our faith, and to trust that God's presence is with us every step of the way.

Throughout her life, Mary's faith continued to be tested and refined. She witnessed the life, ministry, and eventual crucifixion of her Son, enduring unimaginable pain and sorrow. Yet, even in these moments of grief, her faith did not waver. Standing at the foot of the cross, Mary exemplified a faith that endures through suffering, a faith that trusts in God's goodness even in the darkest hours. "Yea, though I walk through the valley of the shadow of death, I will fear no evil: for thou art with me" (Psalm 23:4). Mary's perseverance shows us that faith is not just about believing in the good times; it is about holding on to God's promises in the face of pain and loss. Her journey reminds us that God is with us in every season, comforting and sustaining us through His unending love.

As we look to Mary's example, we see that perseverance in faith is about trusting in God's timing. Mary's life was marked by moments of waiting—waiting for the birth of her Son, waiting as He grew, and waiting as He fulfilled His purpose. Her patience reflects a deep trust in God's perfect timing, a willingness to wait for His plans to unfold. "Wait on the Lord: be of good courage, and he shall strengthen thine heart: wait, I say, on the Lord" (Psalm 27:14). Mary's faith teaches us that waiting is not passive; it is an active trust in God's sovereignty, a surrender to His will, and a confidence that He is working all things together for good.

Mary's song of praise, the Magnificat, is a beautiful expression of her faith and gratitude. "My soul doth magnify the Lord, and my spirit hath rejoiced in God my Saviour. For he hath regarded the low estate of his handmaiden" (Luke 1:46-48). Her words reveal a heart full of worship, a heart that recognizes God's mercy and grace. Mary's praise reflects her deep joy in the Lord, a joy that is rooted in her trust in His promises. Her song is a reminder that faith is not only about obedience but also about rejoicing in God's goodness. Mary's life invites us to lift our voices in praise, to magnify the Lord for His faithfulness, and to find joy in His presence.

In Mary's story, we see that perseverance in faith requires humility. She did not seek recognition or honor; she simply sought to do God's will. Her humility is a reminder that faith is about surrendering our desires and ambitions, choosing instead to follow God's lead. "Humble yourselves therefore under the mighty hand of God, that he may exalt you in due time" (1 Peter 5:6). Mary's example encourages us to embrace humility, to trust that God's plans are greater than our own, and to find peace in knowing that He is in control. Her life reflects a quiet strength, a strength that comes from relying on God and submitting to His authority.

As we celebrate Christmas, Mary's faith calls us to reflect on our own relationship with God. Her willingness to say, "Be it unto me according to thy word" (Luke 1:38), challenges us to examine whether we are truly surrendered to God's will. Mary's faith was not a passive belief but an active commitment to God's purpose. Her example encourages us to live with a heart of obedience, to trust in God's promises, and to persevere in faith, no matter the cost. Mary's journey reminds us that God is faithful, that His plans are good, and that His love is steadfast. Just as she carried the Savior into the world, we are called to carry His love, hope, and joy into our lives, sharing the good news of His coming with others.

Mary's story is a testament to the power of faith, a faith that perseveres through every challenge, a faith that trusts in God's promises, and a faith that rejoices in His presence. This Christmas, as we reflect on her example, may we be inspired to pursue God with the same dedication, to trust Him with the same confidence, and to praise Him with the same joy. Mary's faith invites us to draw near to God, to embrace His will, and to live as faithful servants of His love.

# Chapter 12 – Partnership of Quiet Obedience

In "O Come, Let Us Adore Him: A Christmas Devotional," we find inspiration in the quiet, steadfast obedience of Joseph, a man chosen by God to be part of His divine plan to bring Jesus into the world. Joseph's journey of faith began when he learned of Mary's miraculous pregnancy—a situation that tested his heart, his faith, and his commitment to God's will. As a righteous man, Joseph could have chosen a path that would shield him from judgment or confusion, yet his heart was open to God, and he was willing to listen and obey. When the angel appeared to him in a dream, explaining that Mary's child was conceived by the Holy Spirit, Joseph didn't hesitate to follow God's command. The angel told him, "Joseph, thou son of David, fear not to take unto thee Mary thy wife: for that which is conceived in her is of the Holy Ghost" (Matthew 1:20). Joseph's response to this divine message was one of trust and submission, revealing his willingness to be part of God's redemptive plan. With quiet faithfulness, he accepted his role, setting aside his own doubts, his own plans, and any concerns about what others might say. In his obedience, Joseph shows us the beauty of submission to God, a submission that is not loud or boastful but rooted in deep trust and love for the Lord.

Joseph's obedience highlights the strength found in trusting God's guidance even when circumstances are unclear or challenging. His decision to take Mary as his wife was an act of faith, a partnership with God that would impact the entire course of history. "Then Joseph... did as the angel of the Lord had bidden him, and took unto him his wife" (Matthew 1:24). Joseph's quiet obedience demonstrates a partnership with God's will, a willingness to walk a path filled with uncertainty but also great purpose. In choosing to obey, Joseph embraced his calling, taking on the responsibility of caring for and protecting Jesus as He grew. His role was not to be in the spotlight, but rather to stand by, faithfully supporting the divine work that was unfolding before him. In his obedience, we see a man who humbly chose God's way over his own, reflecting a heart fully surrendered to the Lord.

Through Joseph's example, we are reminded that obedience to God often means putting aside our own understanding and submitting to His greater plan. Joseph didn't have all the answers, but he trusted in God's wisdom and followed where God led him. "Trust in the Lord with all thine heart; and lean not unto thine own understanding. In all thy ways acknowledge him, and he shall direct thy paths" (Proverbs 3:5-6). Joseph's journey invites us to follow God's direction, even when it leads us into the unknown, and to trust that His plans are far greater than anything we could imagine. His obedience teaches us that true partnership with God means walking in faith, taking each step as He leads, and allowing His will to guide our lives.

As Joseph accepted his role in God's plan, he also accepted the responsibility of being a father to Jesus, to love, nurture, and protect the Son of God. His obedience was not only an act of faith but also a demonstration of love and devotion. Joseph cared for Mary and Jesus with unwavering dedication, providing a stable and loving home for the Savior of the world. His commitment to his family reflects the depth of his obedience, a partnership with God that went beyond mere actions and touched the very core of his heart. "And whatsoever ye do, do it heartily, as to the Lord, and not unto men" (Colossians 3:23). Joseph's faithfulness reminds us that obedience to God is an act of worship, a way of expressing our love and gratitude to the One who calls us to walk alongside Him in His purposes.

Throughout his journey, Joseph's obedience was tested, yet he remained faithful to God's call. When the angel appeared to him once more, warning him to flee to Egypt to protect Jesus from King Herod's wrath, Joseph did not question or delay. "When he arose, he took the young child and his mother by night, and departed into Egypt" (Matthew 2:14). His prompt response shows a heart that is fully attuned to God's voice, a heart willing to go wherever God leads, no matter the cost. Joseph's obedience to God's command to flee to Egypt reveals the depth of his commitment, a willingness to sacrifice his own comfort and safety for the sake of protecting Jesus. His actions remind us that obedience to God often requires courage and resilience, a steadfast faith that holds firm even in the face of danger or difficulty.

In Joseph's life, we see a beautiful partnership with God—a partnership built on trust, love, and obedience. His role may not have been one of fame or recognition, but it was essential to the unfolding of God's plan. Joseph's obedience teaches us that true greatness in God's kingdom is found not in seeking our own glory but in faithfully serving His purpose. His example encourages us to embrace our roles, no matter how small or unseen they may seem, and to trust that God is using our obedience to accomplish His will. "Humble yourselves therefore under the mighty hand of God, that he may exalt you in due time" (1 Peter 5:6). Joseph's quiet faithfulness reveals the beauty of humility, a willingness to lay down our own desires and ambitions to follow the path God has set before us.

As we reflect on Joseph's obedience, we are reminded that God values our willingness to listen and respond to His call. Joseph's life shows us that obedience is not always about understanding every detail of God's plan but about trusting in His goodness and walking in faith. "For we walk by faith, not by sight" (2 Corinthians 5:7). Joseph's journey encourages us to take each step with confidence in God's promises, knowing that He is guiding us and that His plans are perfect. His faithfulness to God's call is an example for us all, a reminder that our obedience to God reflects our love and trust in Him.

In Joseph's partnership with God, we see the importance of being attentive to His voice and willing to follow wherever He leads. Joseph's obedience was not marked by grand gestures but by simple, faithful actions—taking Mary as his wife, protecting Jesus, and providing for his family. His life reminds us that God calls us to be faithful in the everyday moments, to honor Him in our daily decisions, and to seek His will in all things. "And whatsoever ye do in word or deed, do all in the name of the Lord Jesus, giving thanks to God and the Father by him" (Colossians 3:17). Joseph's quiet obedience reveals the power of a life dedicated to God's purposes, a life that honors Him in both big and small ways.

This Christmas, as we celebrate the birth of Jesus, let us be inspired by Joseph's obedience, his quiet partnership with God, and his willingness to follow wherever God led him. May his example encourage us to embrace our roles in God's plan with the same faith, humility, and dedication. Joseph's life shows us that obedience to God is not about seeking recognition or reward but about trusting in His love and serving Him with all our hearts. His story invites us to join in God's purposes, to walk in partnership with Him, and to find joy in following His lead. Just as Joseph cared for Jesus with love and devotion, may we also serve God with a heart of obedience, trusting that He is using our lives to accomplish His will and bring glory to His name.

# Chapter 13 – Pathway of Divine Light

In "O Come, Let Us Adore Him: A Christmas Devotional," the story of the Star of Bethlehem reminds us of the divine guidance God provides to lead us to His Son, Jesus Christ. The wise men, or Magi, who traveled from the East, were drawn to the star, knowing that it symbolized the birth of a King like no other. Their journey was not an ordinary one; it was a pursuit of hope, a response to a divine sign that called them to follow and find the promised Savior. When they saw the star in the sky, they said, "We have seen his star in the east, and are come to worship him" (Matthew 2:2). This star, shining brightly in the night sky, was a pathway set by God to guide them directly to Jesus. They were filled with determination, their hearts set on honoring the One whom the star proclaimed. The Star of Bethlehem is a symbol of God's faithfulness to direct our paths and illuminate the way to Him, a reminder that even in the darkest nights, God provides a light to guide us closer to His presence.

Just as the star led the wise men, God's guidance leads us on a pathway of faith, helping us to seek Jesus with all our hearts. The star was not only a celestial sign; it was an invitation, a beacon of hope drawing the wise men closer to the Savior. Their journey was long and filled with unknowns, but they trusted in the light that God had provided, knowing that it would lead them to something greater than they could imagine. "Thy word is a lamp unto my feet, and a light unto my path" (Psalm 119:105). The journey of the wise men shows us that when we follow God's guidance, even when the path is unclear, we are led to the fullness of His love and the beauty of His presence. Their faith in the star's direction is a powerful example of how we are called to trust in God's guidance, knowing that He will faithfully lead us to where we need to be.

The Star of Bethlehem represents God's promise to be with us, to lead us, and to make His presence known in our lives. The wise men's journey is a reminder that God never leaves us to find our way alone; He provides a pathway that leads directly to Him. "The steps of a good man are ordered by the Lord: and he delighteth in his way" (Psalm 37:23). Just as He placed the star in the sky for the wise men to follow, God places signs and guidance in our lives, calling us to pursue Him with a heart of worship and wonder. The star was a light that broke through the darkness, symbolizing the hope and salvation that Jesus would bring to the world. It shines as a reminder that God's love reaches us even when we are far away, drawing us near to Him and revealing His presence in ways we might not expect.

The wise men's journey was one of worship and adoration, a journey that culminated in their encounter with the Savior. They followed the star with a heart set on honoring Jesus, bringing gifts of gold, frankincense, and myrrh to lay at His feet. Their journey was not simply about seeing the King; it was about offering themselves in humble worship. "When they were come into the house, they saw the young child with Mary his mother, and fell down, and worshipped him" (Matthew 2:11). The wise men's response to the star's guidance was one of reverence, a reminder that when God leads us, our ultimate destination is a place of worship. Their journey calls us to approach Jesus with the same awe and humility, to bring the gift of our hearts and lives before Him, and to adore the One who came to bring light to the world.

The star's light shone in the night, guiding the wise men through the darkness, a symbol of God's unwavering guidance in our own lives. In times when the path ahead seems unclear, God's light is there to direct us, to show us the way, and to reassure us that He is with us. "The Lord shall guide thee continually" (Isaiah 58:11). The journey of the wise men encourages us to trust in God's guidance, to believe that even when we cannot see the whole picture, He is leading us closer to His heart. The star of Bethlehem serves as a reminder that God's plans are purposeful, that He is always at work, and that His light will never fail to lead us to His presence.

The Star of Bethlehem also symbolizes hope—a hope that shines brightly in a world often filled with uncertainty. Just as the wise men found hope in the star, we find hope in knowing that God has a purpose for our lives, that He is guiding us toward His promises. "For I know the thoughts that I think toward you, saith the Lord, thoughts of peace, and not of evil, to give you an expected end" (Jeremiah 29:11). The star reassures us that God is with us, that He is lighting the way before us, and that we are never alone. This hope is the anchor of our souls, a reminder that as we follow His guidance, we will find peace, joy, and the fulfillment of His promises.

The story of the wise men and the Star of Bethlehem is a reminder of the beauty and wonder of seeking Jesus. They journeyed from afar, overcoming distance and obstacles, to worship the King. Their pursuit of Jesus teaches us the importance of seeking Him with all our hearts, of following the light that God places in our lives, and of trusting in His guidance along the way. "Seek ye the Lord while he may be found, call ye upon him while he is near" (Isaiah 55:6). The wise men's journey calls us to pursue Jesus with the same dedication and determination, to seek Him as our greatest treasure, and to worship Him as the King of kings.

As we reflect on the Star of Bethlehem, we are reminded of God's faithfulness to lead us to Jesus, to guide us on a pathway that draws us closer to His love and grace. The wise men's journey encourages us to trust in God's timing, to follow His lead, and to believe that He is guiding us to something greater than we can understand. Their pursuit of the star shows us that God's guidance is a gift, a light that shines in the darkness, leading us to the joy and peace found in His presence. "For with thee is the fountain of life: in thy light shall we see light" (Psalm 36:9). The star is a symbol of the light of Christ, a light that brings clarity to our path and fills our hearts with hope.

The Star of Bethlehem reminds us that God's guidance is constant and unchanging. Just as the wise men followed the star to Jesus, we are called to follow His light, to trust in His direction, and to let His presence lead us each day. "I am the light of the world: he that followeth me shall not walk in darkness, but shall have the light of life" (John 8:12). The star's light is a reminder that Jesus is the true light, the One who guides us through life's challenges and leads us to the peace and joy of knowing Him. The wise men's journey to Bethlehem shows us that when we follow God's guidance, we are drawn into His presence, where we find the fullness of joy and the hope of salvation.

The story of the Star of Bethlehem is a call to trust in God's faithfulness, to believe that He is guiding us even when the path is unclear, and to follow His light with a heart of worship. The wise men's journey is an example of faith, a reminder that God's guidance is a pathway to His presence. As we follow the light that He provides, we are led to Jesus, the source of true peace, hope, and joy. This Christmas, let us be inspired by the Star of Bethlehem, let us seek Jesus with all our hearts, and let us trust in the guidance of God's unfailing light.

# Chapter 14 – Pursuit of Reverent Adoration

In "O Come, Let Us Adore Him: A Christmas Devotional," we are inspired by the profound worship of the wise men, the Magi, who journeyed from afar to honor the newborn King, demonstrating that Jesus is truly worthy of adoration from all nations and peoples. The wise men, led by a star, followed God's divine guidance across vast lands and through uncertain paths, all with the purpose of worshipping the Savior, the one who had come to bring light and salvation to the world. Upon reaching Bethlehem and entering the house, their journey culminated in a beautiful moment of reverence as "they saw the young child with Mary his mother, and fell down, and worshipped him" (Matthew 2:11). The sight of Jesus, though a humble child, moved them to kneel and bow in awe, their hearts overflowing with gratitude, humility, and joy. Their worship was not casual or obligatory but heartfelt and genuine, born out of the recognition that this child was unlike any other. He was Emmanuel, God with us, the promised Messiah whose love and grace would redeem humanity. The Magi's journey and worship illustrate the deep praise and reverence that Jesus deserves from all, a reminder that the worth of our Lord surpasses boundaries, cultures, and nations, calling each of us to bring our hearts in adoration before Him.

The wise men's worship reflects a powerful message of humility and reverence. Despite being men of knowledge, wealth, and status, they set aside their own importance to honor Jesus, demonstrating that true worship comes from a heart willing to bow before God, acknowledging Him as Lord. "O come, let us worship and bow down: let us kneel before the Lord our maker" (Psalm 95:6). Their act of falling down before Jesus teaches us that worship is not about seeking recognition but about humbly offering ourselves to God, exalting Him above all else. The wise men's reverence reminds us that the only response to the majesty and holiness of Christ is to bow in adoration, to surrender ourselves fully to His love and sovereignty.

As the wise men offered their gifts—gold, frankincense, and myrrh—they symbolized the honor and praise that Jesus, the King of Kings, rightfully deserves. Each gift represented an aspect of who Jesus is: gold for His kingship, frankincense for His divinity, and myrrh as a symbol of His coming sacrifice. These offerings were not merely tokens but acts of deep significance, reflecting their understanding of the Messiah's role in their lives and in the world. "Give unto the Lord the glory due unto his name: bring an offering, and come before him: worship the Lord in the beauty of holiness" (1 Chronicles 16:29). Their gifts were an expression of their praise, a recognition that Jesus was worthy of the finest treasures they could bring. The wise men's offerings remind us that our worship, too, should be generous, heartfelt, and given with love, for our Savior is worthy of our best.

The journey of the Magi was one marked by faith, determination, and a longing to worship the King. They traveled long distances, undeterred by the obstacles and unknowns before them, driven by a desire to honor Jesus. Their worship was not convenient; it required sacrifice and perseverance, showing that true praise often involves setting aside our own comfort and embracing the pursuit of God with our whole hearts. "Seek the Lord and his strength, seek his face continually" (1 Chronicles 16:11). Their journey calls us to worship with the same passion and commitment, to pursue Jesus with hearts full of faith, and to offer Him the praise that He is due.

In the presence of Jesus, the wise men experienced a joy that was beyond anything the world could offer. The Bible tells us that when they saw the star leading them to the Savior, "they rejoiced with exceeding great joy" (Matthew 2:10). Their worship was filled with a joy that came from knowing they were in the presence of the King, a joy that overflowed from their hearts as they knelt before Him. This joy is a reminder that true worship fills us with a peace and happiness that only God can give. The wise men's journey and worship show us that when we seek Jesus, when we bring our hearts in praise before Him, we find a joy that transcends our circumstances, a joy that fills our souls with hope and love.

The story of the Magi is a reminder that Jesus is the Savior for all people, that His love and grace reach beyond borders and invite everyone to worship.

The wise men were foreigners, yet they recognized the significance of Christ's birth and came to honor Him, showing that worship is universal, a gift given to people from every nation and background. "For mine eyes have seen thy salvation, which thou hast prepared before the face of all people; a light to lighten the Gentiles, and the glory of thy people Israel" (Luke 2:30-32). Their worship is a powerful testimony that Jesus is the light of the world, the hope for all, inviting each of us to come and adore Him, regardless of where we come from or who we are.

As we reflect on the wise men's worship, we are reminded that our lives, too, are meant to be offerings of praise to God. Worship is not limited to a single moment; it is a way of life, an ongoing expression of love and gratitude to our Savior. The wise men's act of worship encourages us to live each day with a heart of praise, to let our actions, words, and lives reflect the adoration we have for Jesus. "I will bless the Lord at all times: his praise shall continually be in my mouth" (Psalm 34:1). Their story invites us to worship Jesus not only with our words but with our whole being, offering our lives as a living sacrifice to honor Him.

In their worship, the wise men remind us of the beauty of surrender, of laying down our own desires to seek the will of God. They came not to receive but to give, to bow in humility before the One who is worthy of all praise. "Worthy is the Lamb that was slain to receive power, and riches, and wisdom, and strength, and honour, and glory, and blessing" (Revelation 5:12). Their worship challenges us to approach Jesus with the same heart of surrender, to give Him all that we are, knowing that He is worthy of our adoration and trust.

The Magi's journey and worship are an invitation to experience the wonder and awe of being in God's presence. As they knelt before Jesus, they were filled with a reverence and joy that comes from encountering the divine. This Christmas, may we be inspired by the wise men's worship, may we seek Jesus with all our hearts, and may we bring our praise to the One who is worthy of all honor and glory. Their story reminds us that Jesus is our King, our Savior, and our greatest treasure, and He is worthy of all our praise.

# Chapter 15 – Presentation of Profound Devotion

In "O Come, Let Us Adore Him: A Christmas Devotional," the moment the wise men presented their gifts to Jesus reveals a powerful message about honoring Him as King, Priest, and Savior, with gifts that acknowledge His divine purpose. When the wise men traveled from afar, they came prepared to offer something precious, a presentation of their love, faith, and understanding of who Jesus truly was. "And when they were come into the house, they saw the young child with Mary his mother, and fell down, and worshipped him: and when they had opened their treasures, they presented unto him gifts; gold, and frankincense, and myrrh" (Matthew 2:11). These gifts were not chosen at random; each one carried deep symbolic meaning, reflecting the identity of Jesus and the roles He would fulfill in His life and ministry. Gold, a gift fit for a king, represented His royal lineage and His reign as the King of Kings, the one who would rule with justice, love, and truth. Frankincense, a precious incense used in temple worship, symbolized His role as our High Priest, the one who would intercede on our behalf, bridging the gap between God and humanity. Myrrh, an aromatic spice used for anointing and burial, foreshadowed His sacrificial death, acknowledging Him as the Savior who would lay down His life to redeem us from sin. Each gift was a presentation of the highest honor, a recognition of Jesus' divine purpose, and an act of worship that pointed to His eternal significance.

The wise men's gifts remind us that Jesus is worthy of our best, that in Him we find the fulfillment of every promise and the answer to every longing. "For unto us a child is born, unto us a son is given: and the government shall be upon his shoulder: and his name shall be called Wonderful, Counsellor, The mighty God, The everlasting Father, The Prince of Peace" (Isaiah 9:6). The wise men's offerings reflect their understanding of Jesus' identity, showing us that true worship involves giving what is most valuable to honor the greatness of who He is. Gold for His kingship tells us that Jesus is not only our Savior but also the Lord of our lives, deserving of our loyalty, reverence, and submission. Frankincense for His priesthood reveals that Jesus is our advocate, our intercessor, the one who prays for us and draws us close to the heart of God. Myrrh for His sacrifice reminds us that Jesus came to give His life, to endure suffering on our behalf, that we might be reconciled to God. Each gift was a presentation of their deepest respect and devotion, a way of acknowledging that Jesus held the highest place in their hearts and lives.

In presenting these gifts, the wise men gave not only from their material wealth but from the richness of their faith, showing us that true worship is about offering our hearts fully to Jesus. Their journey was long and filled with challenges, yet they traveled with unwavering purpose, determined to honor the newborn King with gifts that symbolized their understanding and love for Him. "Where your treasure is, there will your heart be also" (Matthew 6:21). Their treasures were not simply physical gifts; they were expressions of their adoration and belief in Jesus. The wise men's gifts encourage us to offer what is most valuable in our own lives, to lay down our fears, our desires, and our ambitions, and to give Jesus the highest place in our hearts. Gold, frankincense, and myrrh teach us that worship is not about the quantity of our gifts but the quality of our devotion, the sincerity of our love, and the willingness to present ourselves wholly to the One who is worthy.

The act of giving these gifts also shows us the depth of the wise men's understanding of who Jesus was and what He would accomplish. They did not come to Him with ordinary offerings; they brought gifts that pointed to His eternal purpose. Gold represented His majesty and authority as the King of Kings, affirming that Jesus came to establish a kingdom of righteousness and peace. "He shall reign over the house of Jacob for ever; and of his kingdom there shall be no end" (Luke 1:33). This gift reminds us that Jesus reigns over all, that His authority is unmatched, and that He is worthy of our obedience and reverence. Frankincense, an incense used in worship, signifies His priesthood, His role as the one who would bring us into God's presence and offer prayers on our behalf. "We have not an high priest which cannot be touched with the feeling of our infirmities" (Hebrews 4:15). In Jesus, we find a compassionate and understanding High Priest, one who knows our struggles and intercedes for us with love and mercy. Myrrh, a spice associated with anointing and burial, foretells His suffering and sacrifice, the price He would pay for our redemption. "Greater love hath no man than this, that a man lay down his life for his friends" (John 15:13). Myrrh reminds us that Jesus' love is sacrificial, that He willingly endured the cross to bring us salvation and eternal life.

The wise men's presentation of these gifts is an invitation for us to come before Jesus with a heart of worship, to bring our own offerings of love, faith, and surrender. Just as they opened their treasures, we are called to open our hearts, to give Jesus all that we are and all that we have, trusting that He is worthy of every gift we can bring. "I beseech you therefore, brethren, by the mercies of God, that ye present your bodies a living sacrifice, holy, acceptable unto God, which is your reasonable service" (Romans 12:1). The wise men's example calls us to a life of devotion, to a heart that is willing to sacrifice, and to a spirit that finds joy in giving to the One who gave His all for us.

The story of the wise men and their gifts reminds us that Jesus is the treasure we seek, the One who fulfills our deepest desires and brings peace to our hearts. Their journey to present these gifts was an act of faith, a pursuit of the One who is the source of all joy, hope, and salvation. "For where your treasure is, there will your heart be also" (Luke 12:34). Their gifts teach us that true worship is about more than words; it is about offering our lives to Jesus, laying down our own desires, and finding our greatest fulfillment in Him. The wise men's presentation of gold, frankincense, and myrrh challenges us to consider what we are willing to give, to ask ourselves if Jesus holds the highest place in our hearts, and to recognize that He alone is worthy of our praise and adoration.

In this Christmas season, as we reflect on the wise men's gifts, let us be inspired to come before Jesus with a heart of worship, to present our own gifts of love, gratitude, and devotion. Just as they honored Him with treasures fit for a King, may we honor Him with lives that are fully surrendered, with hearts that seek to glorify Him in all that we do. The wise men's gifts remind us that Jesus is our King, our Priest, and our Savior, the one who deserves the best of what we have to offer. "Unto him be glory and dominion for ever and ever" (Revelation 1:6). This Christmas, let us bring our own gifts to Jesus, gifts that reflect our love, our faith, and our gratitude for all that He has done for us.

# Chapter 16 – Presence of Perpetual Love

In "O Come, Let Us Adore Him: A Christmas Devotional," the name Immanuel, which means "God with us," stands as one of the most powerful and beautiful truths of the Christmas story, a reminder that God Himself has come near to dwell with us in love and compassion. When the angel appeared to Joseph, he brought the message that Mary would bear a son, and they would call Him Immanuel, for through Jesus, God's presence would come to be with His people forever. "Behold, a virgin shall be with child, and shall bring forth a son, and they shall call his name Emmanuel, which being interpreted is, God with us" (Matthew 1:23). In this name, Immanuel, we find the heartbeat of God's love for humanity, His desire to be near us, to walk with us, to comfort us, and to bring us hope and peace in every season. The story of Christmas is not only about a Savior who came to redeem us but about a God who wanted to be close to us, to experience life alongside us, to bear our burdens, to share our joys, and to offer us the warmth of His divine presence each day.

The birth of Jesus brought heaven and earth together, showing us that God is not distant or removed but deeply involved in our lives. "The Lord is nigh unto all them that call upon him, to all that call upon him in truth" (Psalm 145:18). Through Jesus, we have a constant friend, a faithful guide, and a loving Father who is always near. The name Immanuel declares that God is not just watching over us from afar; He is walking beside us, through every joy and trial, through every high and low, holding our hand and sustaining our hearts. In moments of loneliness or struggle, we can find comfort in knowing that God is with us, that He understands our every need, and that He is here to support and strengthen us. "Fear thou not; for I am with thee: be not dismayed; for I am thy God: I will strengthen thee; yea, I will help thee; yea, I will uphold thee with the right hand of my righteousness" (Isaiah 41:10). The presence of God,

Immanuel, reassures us that we are never alone, that His love surrounds us, and that His peace is available to us at all times.

Immanuel means that God's love is not only a distant promise but a present reality, a love that reaches into the deepest parts of our hearts and transforms our lives. Jesus' coming to earth as Immanuel shows us the extent of God's commitment to His people, His willingness to enter into our broken world to bring healing, hope, and restoration. "For God so loved the world, that he gave his only begotten Son, that whosoever believeth in him should not perish, but have everlasting life" (John 3:16). This love is the reason for the season, the gift that we celebrate, the assurance that no matter where we are or what we face, God is with us, guiding us, comforting us, and drawing us closer to His heart. In Jesus, we find the fullness of God's love and grace, a love that is not conditional or fleeting but steadfast and eternal. Immanuel is the reminder that God's love is real, that it is present in every moment, and that it is powerful enough to carry us through life's challenges and uncertainties.

The presence of Immanuel is a source of strength, helping us to face life's difficulties with courage and faith. Knowing that God is with us gives us the confidence to walk through the darkest valleys, to stand firm in the storms, and to trust that He is in control, even when everything around us seems uncertain. "Yea, though I walk through the valley of the shadow of death, I will fear no evil: for thou art with me; thy rod and thy staff they comfort me" (Psalm 23:4). Jesus' presence is our constant reassurance, our anchor in the midst of life's trials, and our hope when we feel weary or overwhelmed. The name Immanuel is a promise that God's presence is not only with us during the good times but also in our moments of pain, sadness, and doubt. His love does not waver, and His companionship does not falter; He is with us, comforting, guiding, and lifting us, giving us the strength to keep going and the peace to trust in His plan.

When we embrace the truth of Immanuel, we begin to see God's hand at work in our daily lives, His presence in both the ordinary and extraordinary moments. Jesus' birth was a declaration that God's kingdom had come to earth, that heaven had drawn near to humanity in a way that would forever change the world. "The Word was made flesh, and dwelt among us, and we beheld his glory, the glory as of the only begotten of the Father, full of grace and truth" (John 1:14). Through Jesus, God has come near, offering us a glimpse of His glory, inviting us into His presence, and reminding us that His love is always within reach. Immanuel is not just a name; it is an invitation to experience the fullness of God's love, to open our hearts to His grace, and to let His presence transform our lives. His nearness gives us the courage to love, the wisdom to live according to His will, and the joy to celebrate each day as a gift from Him.

In Jesus, we see that God's presence is active and alive, a presence that brings healing, joy, and peace to those who seek Him. As Immanuel, Jesus reached out to the broken, healed the sick, and brought hope to the lost, showing us that God's presence is one of compassion and mercy. "Come unto me, all ye that labour and are heavy laden, and I will give you rest" (Matthew 11:28). Through Jesus, we find rest for our souls, comfort for our hearts, and the assurance that God is near, carrying our burdens and offering us a peace that surpasses all understanding. Immanuel means that we do not have to carry life's burdens alone; God is with us, ready to lift us, to comfort us, and to lead us on the path of His love.

The gift of Immanuel is a reminder that God is actively working in our lives, that His presence is a source of guidance and wisdom. In Jesus, we have a friend who is closer than a brother, a Savior who knows our struggles, and a King who reigns with grace and truth. "Lo, I am with you always, even unto the end of the world" (Matthew 28:20). This promise of Immanuel means that God's presence is not limited to one moment in time; it is eternal, faithful, and unchanging. His presence with us is a constant source of encouragement, a reminder that He is our refuge and strength, our helper in times of need, and our peace in every circumstance. The presence of Jesus, Immanuel, fills our lives with hope, helping us to face each day with a heart full of faith and a spirit anchored in His love.

As we celebrate Christmas, the name Immanuel invites us to draw near to God, to open our hearts to His presence, and to remember that He is with us in every moment. The birth of Jesus is the ultimate expression of God's desire to be close to us, to walk alongside us, and to fill our lives with His love. "Draw nigh to God, and he will draw nigh to you" (James 4:8). Immanuel calls us to live with a heart of gratitude, to embrace the truth that God is near, and to find joy in His presence. This Christmas, may we be reminded that God's love is not distant or unreachable; it is here, alive in our hearts, and ready to lead us into the fullness of His grace. Immanuel—God with us—is the greatest gift of all, a gift that assures us of God's unwavering presence and invites us to walk in His love every day.

# Chapter 17 - Protective Providence of God

In "O Come, Let Us Adore Him: A Christmas Devotional," the protection of Christ stands as a beautiful testament to God's sovereign plan and His unfailing love for His Son. From the very beginning, Jesus' life was surrounded by God's careful protection, reminding us of His powerful and ever-present watch over those He loves. When the angel of the Lord appeared to Joseph, warning him of Herod's intent to destroy the child, God was already in action, ensuring that Jesus would be safe from harm. "And when they were departed, behold, the angel of the Lord appeareth to Joseph in a dream, saying, Arise, and take the young child and his mother, and flee into Egypt, and be thou there until I bring thee word: for Herod will seek the young child to destroy him" (Matthew 2:13). This command was not merely a caution; it was a divine intervention, a shield of protection over the Savior, as God guided Joseph to escape the imminent threat with Mary and Jesus. In this moment, we see that God's love is proactive, guarding His purposes with a strength that cannot be shaken. Through the night journey to Egypt, God's hand was upon them, guiding each step, protecting the precious life of the One who would save humanity. This act of protection is a reminder to us all that God is our defender, always moving to protect His children, fulfilling His plans with a faithful love that never fails.

The protection over Jesus' life speaks to the depth of God's commitment to His promises and His ability to work all things for good. In the face of Herod's wrath, a king driven by jealousy and fear, God remained steadfast, His plans unthwarted, His power unmatched. "No weapon that is formed against thee shall prosper" (Isaiah 54:17). Through this assurance, we see that God's protection is not passive; it is active, intentional, and effective, safeguarding the future that He had lovingly designed for Jesus and for each of us. The journey to Egypt might have seemed unexpected or uncertain, but it was part of God's careful orchestration, revealing His wisdom and sovereignty. Just as He provided a safe haven for Jesus, God provides refuge for us in times of trouble, a shelter in the storms, and a fortress in the face of adversity. The story of Jesus' protection reminds us that when God is with us, we are secure, and no earthly power can alter His divine purposes.

In protecting Jesus from Herod's plot, God demonstrated His faithfulness and the unstoppable nature of His plan. Herod's desire to destroy Jesus was a fierce attempt to prevent the fulfillment of God's promises, yet God's protection shielded His Son from harm, keeping Him safe in the midst of danger. "The Lord is my rock, and my fortress, and my deliverer; my God, my strength, in whom I will trust; my buckler, and the horn of my salvation, and my high tower" (Psalm 18:2). Just as God's protection surrounded Jesus, He surrounds us with His strength and His love, ensuring that His purposes for our lives will come to pass. This protection is not merely a shield; it is an assurance that God is in control, that His plans are perfect, and that He is our defender, guarding us against all that would seek to harm us.

The escape to Egypt also reminds us that God's protection often involves guiding us away from danger and leading us into safe places. In His wisdom, He knows the path we must take, the detours we must follow, and the places where we will find refuge. "The steps of a good man are ordered by the Lord: and he delighteth in his way" (Psalm 37:23). Joseph's obedience to God's direction was an act of faith, trusting that God's guidance would lead them to safety. In this, we are reminded that God's protection is not only about shielding us from harm but about leading us on the right path, one that aligns with His will and brings us closer to His promises. The journey to Egypt was not only a means of escape but a testament to God's guiding hand, a reminder that He is always with us, directing our paths and watching over us with a love that is unwavering.

The protection of Christ in His early years also points to the power of God's provision. In the land of Egypt, away from their home and familiar surroundings, God provided for Mary, Joseph, and Jesus, sustaining them until it was safe to return. "But my God shall supply all your need according to his riches in glory by Christ Jesus" (Philippians 4:19). Just as He provided for Jesus, God provides for us, meeting our needs and ensuring that we are cared for, even in unfamiliar or challenging places. His protection includes His provision, a reminder that He will not only shield us from harm but will also supply what we need to fulfill His purposes. Through this story, we see that God's protection is all-encompassing, extending beyond physical safety to include His sustaining grace, His provision, and His love that cares for every detail of our lives.

The story of God's protection over Jesus reminds us that His plans are unstoppable, that His love is unbreakable, and that His presence is unshakeable. Even when threats arise, when fear seeks to take hold, or when we face circumstances beyond our control, we can rest in the assurance that God's protection surrounds us. "The angel of the Lord encampeth round about them that fear him, and delivereth them" (Psalm 34:7). His angels are with us, guarding us, guiding us, and ensuring that His plans for our lives are fulfilled. In Jesus' story, we see that God's protection is a promise that cannot be broken, a promise that is as faithful and sure as His love for us.

The protection of Christ in His early life reflects the protection God extends to each of His children. Just as He watched over Jesus, guiding, shielding, and leading Him, He watches over us with the same care and devotion. "He shall cover thee with his feathers, and under his wings shalt thou trust: his truth shall be thy shield and buckler" (Psalm 91:4). This image of God's protection is one of tenderness and strength, a reminder that we are safe under His wings, that His truth is our defense, and that His love is our refuge. The journey of Mary, Joseph, and Jesus to Egypt is a testament to God's faithfulness, His power, and His commitment to protect those He loves.

As we reflect on the story of Jesus' protection, we are invited to trust in God's ability to guard our lives, to believe that He is our protector, and to find peace in His sovereign care. "The Lord is thy keeper: the Lord is thy shade upon thy right hand" (Psalm 121:5). Just as He kept Jesus safe from Herod's schemes, He keeps us safe, standing as our defender, our shield, and our strength. This Christmas, as we celebrate the birth of Jesus, may we be reminded of God's unfailing protection, His unwavering love, and His promise to be with us, guiding and guarding us every step of the way.

# Chapter 18 – Precious Provision of Grace

In "O Come, Let Us Adore Him: A Christmas Devotional," we are invited to marvel at God's gift to humanity, the precious and incomparable gift of His Son, Jesus Christ, who brings salvation, hope, and eternal life to all who believe. This gift, sent from heaven and wrapped in humility, is the ultimate expression of God's boundless love and grace. "Thanks be unto God for his unspeakable gift" (2 Corinthians 9:15). Jesus is more than a seasonal story or a distant figure; He is the living, breathing expression of God's provision, a Savior sent to meet our deepest needs and restore us to a loving relationship with our Creator. His coming was not a gift that anyone could earn, demand, or imagine. It was a free and unmerited act of love that changes the course of our lives and offers us a future filled with hope and peace. In Jesus, God provided exactly what we needed, for we were lost in sin, separated from the goodness and holiness of God, unable to bridge the gap on our own. "For all have sinned, and come short of the glory of God" (Romans 3:23). Yet, in His mercy and compassion, God looked upon us with love and sent His Son to be the bridge, the way to restore us, the gift that would heal, save, and set us free.

The magnitude of this gift is beyond words, for it is a gift that meets every need of the human heart, a provision for every longing, and a hope that will never fade. Jesus came not just to show us the way to live but to offer Himself as the way, the truth, and the life. "For the wages of sin is death; but the gift of God is eternal life through Jesus Christ our Lord" (Romans 6:23). Through Jesus, we receive the gift of forgiveness, the promise of eternal life, and the joy of knowing that we are forever loved and accepted by God. This gift was given at great cost, for it meant that Jesus would leave the glory of heaven, take on human form, and walk among us, ultimately laying down His life to pay the price for our sins. His birth in a humble manger was the beginning of a journey that would lead Him to the cross, where He would give everything to bring us back to God. This sacrificial love is the heart of the Christmas story, a reminder that God's gift to us is not about what we deserve but about His great love and mercy. "For God so loved the world, that he gave his only begotten Son, that whosoever believeth in him should not perish, but have everlasting life" (John 3:16).

This gift of Jesus is a gift of grace, a gift we could never earn but can only receive with open hearts. The provision of salvation is not something we achieve by our efforts; it is a divine gift, freely given to all who believe. "For by grace are ye saved through faith; and that not of yourselves: it is the gift of God" (Ephesians 2:8). This gift reminds us that we are loved not for what we do but for who we are in God's eyes, cherished and valued as His children. Through Jesus, God provided a way for us to come close to Him, to be forgiven, cleansed, and made new. He opened the door to a relationship that is marked not by fear or judgment but by love, acceptance, and peace. The gift of Jesus brings us into the family of God, giving us a place in His kingdom, a purpose in His plan, and a promise of eternal life with Him.

As we reflect on God's gift to humanity, we are reminded that this gift is one of hope, a light shining in the darkness, a promise that no matter what we face, God is with us and His love will never fail. "In this was manifested the love of God toward us, because that God sent his only begotten Son into the world, that we might live through him" (1 John 4:9). Jesus is the hope that anchors our souls, the assurance that we are not alone, and the promise that God's love is greater than any fear, sorrow, or challenge we may face. His presence in our lives fills us with peace, knowing that we are held in the hands of a loving God who cares for us and will never abandon us. The gift of Jesus is a light that guides us, a joy that fills us, and a peace that comforts us, reminding us that we are forever secure in His love.

The beauty of this gift is that it is available to everyone, regardless of background, status, or past mistakes. Jesus came to seek and save the lost, to offer redemption to the broken, and to extend grace to the weary. "Come unto me, all ye that labour and are heavy laden, and I will give you rest" (Matthew 11:28). The gift of Jesus is an open invitation to come as we are, to lay down our burdens, and to receive the rest, peace, and joy that only He can give. In Him, we find healing for our wounds, strength for our struggles, and comfort for our sorrows. This gift is a reminder that God's love reaches to the farthest places, to the hearts that feel unworthy, to the souls that feel lost, and to the lives that long for purpose and meaning. The gift of Jesus is for all, an invitation to experience the fullness of God's love and to be transformed by His grace.

As we celebrate Christmas, we are reminded that this season is not about the material gifts we exchange but about the greatest gift ever given: the gift of Jesus, who came to bring life, love, and salvation to a world in need. "Every good gift and every perfect gift is from above, and cometh down from the Father of lights" (James 1:17). Jesus is the perfect gift, the expression of God's perfect love, and the fulfillment of His promises. In Him, we find everything we need, for He is our Savior, our Friend, and our Lord. This Christmas, as we unwrap presents and share moments of joy with loved ones, let us remember the gift of Jesus, the gift that fills our hearts with hope and our lives with purpose.

The gift of Jesus is a call to live with gratitude, to embrace the life He offers, and to share His love with others. Just as we have received this gift freely, we are called to extend His love and grace to those around us, to be a light in the world, and to reflect the heart of God. "Freely ye have received, freely give" (Matthew 10:8). This gift is not meant to be kept to ourselves but to be shared, to be a source of blessing, and to bring others into the joy and peace that we have found in Jesus. As we celebrate this season, let us be reminded that we are part of God's story, called to live in His love and to share His gift of salvation with a world in need.

In Jesus, we have been given the greatest gift of all, a gift that fills our lives with love, joy, and hope. This gift is a reminder that God's love is unending, His grace is sufficient, and His promises are true. "The Lord hath appeared of old unto me, saying, Yea, I have loved thee with an everlasting love: therefore with lovingkindness have I drawn thee" (Jeremiah 31:3). This Christmas, may we come before God with grateful hearts, thanking Him for the gift of Jesus, the gift that changed everything and opened the way to eternal life. In Jesus, we find the fullness of God's love, the depth of His mercy, and the joy of being His children.

# Chapter 19 - Piercing Presence of Divine Light

In "O Come, Let Us Adore Him: A Christmas Devotional," we are drawn to the truth of Jesus as the Light of the World, a light so brilliant that it breaks through every darkness, filling our hearts and lives with hope, peace, and clarity. When Jesus declared, "I am the light of the world: he that followeth me shall not walk in darkness, but shall have the light of life" (John 8:12), He was offering us something no one else could—the promise of a light that overcomes every shadow, a light that guides us in times of confusion, a light that brings peace in the midst of turmoil. In a world often filled with uncertainty and fear, Jesus' light is a constant, unwavering presence that assures us of His love and the truth of His promises. From the beginning, God intended for us to live in the light, for "God is light, and in him is no darkness at all" (1 John 1:5). Jesus came to shine this divine light into the world, to illuminate the way back to God, and to offer us a life filled with the warmth and assurance of His presence. His light is like no other; it is a light that heals, a light that reveals, and a light that transforms.

When we encounter Jesus, we encounter the brilliance of God's love—a light so pure and radiant that it reveals the truth of who we are and leads us into a deeper relationship with our Creator. This light is not merely a guide; it is a source of life, filling us with joy and strength as we walk in its glow. "The Lord is my light and my salvation; whom shall I fear?" (Psalm 27:1). Jesus, the Light of the World, shines into the darkest corners of our lives, driving out fear, shame, and doubt. He replaces our anxieties with His peace, our sorrows with His joy, and our uncertainties with the firm foundation of His truth. His light is a comfort, reminding us that no matter how dark the world may seem, His presence is with us, illuminating our path and filling our hearts with the assurance that we are never alone.

The coming of Jesus as the Light of the World is a gift that reveals God's desire to draw us close, to bring us out of the darkness of sin and into the brightness of His love and forgiveness. "To give light to them that sit in darkness and in the shadow of death, to guide our feet into the way of peace" (Luke 1:79). Jesus came to lift us from the shadows, to show us the beauty of a life lived in communion with God, and to guide us along a path filled with purpose and peace. His light is a beacon of hope, a reminder that God's love reaches us even in the deepest despair, offering us a way forward when we feel lost or broken. This light is a constant, shining brightly through every storm, reminding us that with Jesus, we have a hope that will never fade.

In every moment, Jesus' light is there to guide, protect, and encourage us. When we feel overwhelmed or unsure, His light shines on the path before us, giving us the courage to move forward in faith. "Thy word is a lamp unto my feet, and a light unto my path" (Psalm 119:105). The light of Jesus is like a guiding star, leading us through life's challenges, showing us the way of love, kindness, and forgiveness. This light calls us to live in a way that reflects His goodness, to be lights ourselves in a world that needs His love and truth. Jesus doesn't just illuminate our lives; He transforms us into bearers of His light, inviting us to shine with the same love, compassion, and grace that He so freely offers.

Through His light, Jesus exposes the lies that would keep us bound, freeing us from the chains of sin and fear. His light is a purifying force, refining our hearts, shaping our character, and calling us to live in holiness. "But if we walk in the light, as he is in the light, we have fellowship one with another, and the blood of Jesus Christ his Son cleanseth us from all sin" (1 John 1:7). Walking in the light means choosing to live with integrity, to love others as He loves us, and to seek truth in all things. Jesus' light transforms our relationships, bringing healing and restoration, teaching us to forgive, and helping us to build bonds of unity and peace. His light is a gift that renews us daily, giving us the strength to rise above our struggles and to live each day in the joy and freedom of His love.

The light of Jesus also reminds us of the promise of eternity, a future where darkness will be no more, where we will dwell in His presence forever. "And there shall be no night there; and they need no candle, neither light of the sun; for the Lord God giveth them light" (Revelation 22:5). In His light, we find the assurance that death is not the end, that God has prepared a place for us where we will experience the fullness of His glory. This hope gives us strength in the face of life's challenges, a steadfast confidence that we are part of something greater, a kingdom that will never fade. Jesus' light gives us a glimpse of this heavenly reality, a foretaste of the joy and peace that await us. His light is a promise, a guarantee that His love will carry us into eternity, where we will forever be in the presence of His glory.

As we reflect on Jesus as the Light of the World, we are reminded that this light is not just for us but for everyone. His love extends to all, and we are called to share this light with those around us, to reflect His love in our words, actions, and lives. "Ye are the light of the world. A city that is set on a hill cannot be hid" (Matthew 5:14). Jesus invites us to carry His light into the world, to be a beacon of hope, a source of encouragement, and a testimony to the power of His love. When we live in His light, we shine with a radiance that can't be hidden, a joy that draws others to the truth of His grace. His light in us becomes a gift to others, an invitation to experience the same love, peace, and salvation that we have found in Him.

In this season, as we celebrate the birth of Jesus, let us remember that He is the true light that dispels every shadow, that brings warmth to every heart, and that offers guidance in every season. His light is a constant presence, a reminder of God's love that surrounds us and sustains us. "The people that walked in darkness have seen a great light: they that dwell in the land of the shadow of death, upon them hath the light shined" (Isaiah 9:2). This Christmas, may we open our hearts to receive the light of Jesus, allowing it to fill every corner of our lives, to chase away every fear, and to bring us closer to Him. In Jesus, we have been given a gift that will never fade, a light that will never dim, a hope that will never disappoint.

# Chapter 20 – Portrait of Pure Joy

In "O Come, Let Us Adore Him: A Christmas Devotional," the message of "Joy to the World" resounds with hope, love, and celebration, inviting all people to rejoice because Christ, the Savior, has come. His birth is a gift that brings joy beyond measure, a joy that fills our hearts and calls all of creation to celebrate. As the Psalmist proclaimed, "Let the heavens rejoice, and let the earth be glad" (Psalm 96:11), we see that this joy is not confined to one time or place; it is a joy that reaches to the heavens and fills the earth. This is the joy of knowing that God Himself has come near to us, that He has fulfilled His promises and brought salvation to a world in need. The birth of Jesus is a declaration of God's love, a reminder that He has come to save us, to bring light into our darkness, and to fill our lives with peace and purpose. This joy is not merely an emotion; it is a deep, abiding gladness that comes from knowing that we are loved, valued, and redeemed by the Creator of the universe. "Thou hast put gladness in my heart" (Psalm 4:7), and this gladness overflows because in Jesus, we have found our reason to celebrate, our hope in times of trouble, and our assurance that we are never alone.

Christ's birth invites everyone—people of every nation, age, and background—to rejoice, to come before Him with hearts full of praise and thanksgiving. The joy that Jesus brings is for all who would receive it, a universal invitation to find peace, love, and grace in His presence. "And the angel said unto them, Fear not: for, behold, I bring you good tidings of great joy, which shall be to all people" (Luke 2:10). This great joy is the good news that Jesus has come to bridge the gap between God and humanity, to open the way for us to experience God's love firsthand. In Christ, we are welcomed into a relationship with God that brings joy beyond anything this world can offer. His birth is the fulfillment of prophecies, the answer to our deepest longings, and the beginning of a story that leads to eternal life. This Christmas, as we reflect on the joy of Christ's birth, we are reminded that our Savior's love is personal, powerful, and reaches every heart that is open to Him.

The joy that Jesus brings is not dependent on our circumstances; it is a joy that remains steadfast even in the face of trials. This joy is rooted in the truth that God is with us, that He is our Emmanuel, the one who has come to walk with us, to comfort us, and to guide us. "The Lord thy God in the midst of thee is mighty; he will save, he will rejoice over thee with joy; he will rest in his love, he will joy over thee with singing" (Zephaniah 3:17). Our joy comes from knowing that God delights in us, that He is pleased to dwell among us, and that His presence brings peace to our hearts. This joy reflects His love, a love that does not change with the seasons but remains constant and unchanging. In the birth of Jesus, we see the heart of God, His desire to be near us, to share in our lives, and to fill us with a joy that cannot be shaken.

The joy of Christmas is also a reminder of the victory that Jesus has won for us, the assurance that He has overcome the world and made a way for us to live in freedom and peace. "These things have I spoken unto you, that my joy might remain in you, and that your joy might be full" (John 15:11). Jesus desires for us to live in His joy, to experience a life that is full and complete, a life that is rooted in His love and grounded in His promises. This joy gives us strength, helping us to face each day with courage, to overcome our fears, and to trust in His faithfulness. As we celebrate His birth, we are reminded that joy is a gift that we can carry with us, a light that shines in the darkness, a hope that endures through every trial.

The joy that Jesus brings calls us to share this gift with others, to spread His love, and to be a light in a world that so desperately needs it. Just as the angels proclaimed the good news to the shepherds, we are called to share the message of hope and joy that Jesus brings. "Go ye into all the world, and preach the gospel to every creature" (Mark 16:15). This joy is not meant to be kept to ourselves; it is a gift that grows as we share it, a blessing that multiplies as we bring it to others. When we live with joy, we become witnesses of God's love, reflections of His grace, and bearers of His light. The joy of Christmas is an invitation to be part of God's story, to carry His love into our communities, our families, and our world, bringing hope and healing wherever we go.

As we sing songs of praise and lift our hearts in worship, we join the chorus of angels, the celebration of shepherds, and the adoration of wise men, all who rejoiced at the birth of the Savior. "O come, let us sing unto the Lord: let us make a joyful noise to the rock of our salvation" (Psalm 95:1). Christmas is a time to rejoice, to celebrate the wonder of God's love, and to remember that in Jesus, we have found a joy that is eternal. This joy is a reminder that God's love is real, that His promises are true, and that His presence is with us always. Let us come before Him with hearts full of praise, lifting our voices to declare that Jesus is Lord, that His love is our hope, and that His joy is our strength.

In the birth of Jesus, we find the joy of knowing that we are loved unconditionally, that we are forgiven completely, and that we are held securely in the hands of our Creator. "In thy presence is fulness of joy; at thy right hand there are pleasures for evermore" (Psalm 16:11). This joy is a gift that fills our hearts with peace, that lifts our spirits, and that reminds us of the beauty of God's love. In Jesus, we have found our reason to rejoice, our source of hope, and our everlasting joy. This Christmas, may we open our hearts to the fullness of His love, may we celebrate the wonder of His birth, and may we live each day in the joy that only He can bring.

# Chapter 21 – Pastoral Compassion Personified

In "O Come, Let Us Adore Him: A Christmas Devotional," we look upon Jesus as our Great Shepherd, the one who lovingly guides, protects, and lays down His life for us, His sheep. When Jesus declared, "I am the good shepherd: the good shepherd giveth his life for the sheep" (John 10:11), He was revealing His deep commitment and care for each of us, showing us that He is not a distant or indifferent leader but one who knows us intimately, loves us sacrificially, and leads us with tender compassion. As the Good Shepherd, Jesus is dedicated to watching over us, guarding us from harm, and guiding us through every valley and every shadow. His heart is full of love for His flock, and He goes before us to ensure that we are safe, well-fed, and cared for. "The Lord is my shepherd; I shall not want" (Psalm 23:1). In this beautiful role, Jesus provides for our every need, calming our fears, healing our wounds, and leading us to green pastures where we find rest for our souls. His care is gentle and constant, a reminder that we are never alone, for He is always near, guiding us with His wisdom, strength, and endless love.

As our Great Shepherd, Jesus knows each of us by name, and He calls us personally, inviting us to follow Him on a path of peace, truth, and grace. "My sheep hear my voice, and I know them, and they follow me" (John 10:27). He knows our fears, our struggles, our joys, and our hopes, and He leads us with a love that is patient, understanding, and unwavering. Unlike a hired hand who might abandon the sheep in times of danger, Jesus stays with us, protecting us from every threat, carrying us through every trial, and comforting us when we feel lost or weary. His voice is gentle and reassuring, calling us back when we wander, lifting us up when we stumble, and leading us forward with a heart full of compassion. In His presence, we find peace, knowing that He is guiding us on a path that leads to life, hope, and joy.

Jesus, our Great Shepherd, is also the one who protects us from harm, standing guard over our lives and defending us against the forces of darkness. "Yea, though I walk through the valley of the shadow of death, I will fear no evil: for thou art with me; thy rod and thy staff they comfort me" (Psalm 23:4). His rod and staff are symbols of His strength and guidance, tools that He uses to fend off dangers, to keep us on the right path, and to lead us toward His goodness and mercy. Even when we face difficulties, uncertainties, or fears, we can trust that Jesus is there, walking beside us, ensuring that we are safe, and providing the comfort of His presence. His love for us is unbreakable, a love that will never abandon us or leave us vulnerable. Jesus' care as our Shepherd is a promise that we are never alone, that we are held securely in His hands, and that His love will protect and guide us always.

As the Good Shepherd, Jesus laid down His life for us, proving the depth of His love and the greatness of His sacrifice. "Greater love hath no man than this, that a man lay down his life for his friends" (John 15:13). He did not hesitate to give everything for us, to face suffering and death so that we might have life, peace, and freedom. His sacrifice is the ultimate act of love, a demonstration that He values us beyond measure, that He cherishes each of us as His own. Through His death and resurrection, Jesus has opened the way to eternal life, showing us that His love is stronger than death, that His grace is sufficient for every need, and that His mercy is new each day. In Jesus, we find a Shepherd who is willing to go to any length to rescue us, to bring us back into His fold, and to ensure that we are safe in His love forever.

The Great Shepherd not only cares for us but also leads us to places of spiritual nourishment, filling our souls with His word, refreshing our spirits with His presence, and strengthening us with His truth. "He maketh me to lie down in green pastures: he leadeth me beside the still waters. He restoreth my soul" (Psalm 23:2-3). Jesus knows what we need, and He provides abundantly, ensuring that we are spiritually fed, refreshed, and restored. In His pastures, we find peace, in His waters, we find refreshment, and in His presence, we find healing. His care for us is not only about meeting our physical needs but about nurturing our spirits, guiding us into a deeper relationship with Him, and filling us with His joy and peace.

As our Shepherd, Jesus also seeks us when we are lost, going after the one sheep that has strayed, rejoicing when He finds us and bringing us back into His fold. "What man of you, having an hundred sheep, if he lose one of them, doth not leave the ninety and nine in the wilderness, and go after that which is lost, until he find it?" (Luke 15:4). His love is relentless, a love that never gives up, a love that pursues us with grace and mercy, no matter how far we may wander. Jesus' heart is filled with joy each time one of His lost sheep is found, a reminder that we are precious to Him, that we are worth searching for, and that His love knows no limits. He brings us back with joy, heals our wounds, and restores us to His loving care, proving that His love is greater than our mistakes, stronger than our fears, and deeper than any darkness we may face.

In Jesus, our Great Shepherd, we find a leader who is gentle yet strong, compassionate yet powerful, one who leads us with wisdom and grace. "For ye were as sheep going astray; but are now returned unto the Shepherd and Bishop of your souls" (1 Peter 2:25). He guides us in righteousness, leading us on paths that bring glory to His name, paths that lead us closer to His heart and His purposes for our lives. His leadership is not one of force or control but of love, care, and respect for our hearts. He walks with us, teaches us, and helps us to grow in faith, encouraging us to trust Him more deeply and to follow Him with all our hearts.

As we reflect on Jesus as our Great Shepherd, we are reminded that His love for us is boundless, His care is constant, and His presence is our greatest comfort. He is the Shepherd who knows our hearts, who understands our needs, and who leads us with a love that is tender, patient, and true. In every season, in every challenge, Jesus is there, guiding us, protecting us, and filling us with His peace. His love is a shelter in times of trouble, a light in times of darkness, and a joy in times of sorrow. The heart of our Shepherd is one of compassion, kindness, and mercy, a heart that rejoices in our joys, that comforts us in our sorrows, and that walks beside us every step of the way.

This Christmas, as we celebrate the birth of our Savior, let us remember that Jesus is our Great Shepherd, the one who came to lead us, to care for us, and to bring us into the fold of His everlasting love. Let us come before Him with hearts full of gratitude, trusting in His care, rejoicing in His presence, and following Him wherever He leads. For in Jesus, we have found a Shepherd who is faithful, loving, and true, a Shepherd who gave His life for us, and a Shepherd who will never leave us nor forsake us.

# Chapter 22 – Provision of Spiritual Nourishment

In "O Come, Let Us Adore Him: A Christmas Devotional," we encounter Jesus as the Bread of Life, the One who nourishes our souls and fills the deepest hunger of our hearts. When He declared, "I am the bread of life: he that cometh to me shall never hunger; and he that believeth on me shall never thirst" (John 6:35), Jesus was offering Himself as the sustenance we need to truly live, the source of spiritual strength that fills our emptiness and brings lasting satisfaction. His presence is like bread to the soul, nourishing us in ways that nothing else can. Just as bread is essential for physical life, Jesus is essential for our spiritual lives, providing what our hearts need to grow, to be healed, and to find peace. In Him, we discover the fullness of life, the joy of being known and loved by God, and the strength to face each day with hope. His words are food for our souls, a daily provision that renews, restores, and refreshes us, teaching us that in His love, we are complete. "Man shall not live by bread alone, but by every word that proceedeth out of the mouth of God" (Matthew 4:4). Jesus, our Bread of Life, satisfies a hunger that the world cannot fill, a hunger for purpose, for belonging, and for connection with our Creator.

Jesus' role as the Bread of Life reminds us that He is the true source of life, the One who sustains us through every season, and the One who satisfies our longing for something more. "He hath filled the hungry with good things" (Luke 1:53). This divine provision is not something we can earn or achieve; it is a gift of grace, offered freely to those who come to Him with open hearts and a willingness to receive. In Jesus, we find a love that never fades, a peace that cannot be shaken, and a joy that fills us with strength. Just as bread nourishes the body, Jesus nourishes our spirits, giving us what we need to grow in faith, to overcome life's challenges, and to live with purpose and peace. His presence fills the emptiness, heals the brokenness, and brings us into a place of rest, where we know that we are loved, valued, and sustained by the Creator of all things.

As the Bread of Life, Jesus invites us to come to Him daily, to find our sustenance in His words, His promises, and His presence. "Give us this day our daily bread" (Matthew 6:11). This daily dependence on Jesus teaches us to trust in God's faithfulness, to rely on His provision, and to find our satisfaction in Him alone. Each day, we are invited to partake of His love, to be strengthened by His grace, and to be renewed by His Spirit. In coming to Jesus, we find the sustenance that fills our hearts with joy, our minds with peace, and our lives with purpose. He is our constant source of strength, the One who walks with us through every trial, who lifts us up when we are weary, and who fills us with His love in ways that satisfy our deepest longings.

The Bread of Life is not just about filling our own needs; it is also about sharing this gift with others, offering the love and grace we have received to those around us. "For we being many are one bread, and one body: for we are all partakers of that one bread" (1 Corinthians 10:17). As we are nourished by Jesus, we are called to be His hands and feet in the world, to share His love with those who hunger for hope, peace, and healing. The gift of Jesus, the Bread of Life, transforms us, teaching us to live with compassion, to reach out with kindness, and to offer a message of hope to a world in need. His love fills us so that we can overflow with His grace, spreading the light of His love and bringing His peace to those who need it most.

In Jesus, we find a bread that never spoils, a provision that never runs out, and a love that never fades. His presence is our sustenance, our strength, and our hope, a daily reminder that we are held in the hands of a loving and faithful God. "I am that bread of life" (John 6:48). In this season of Christmas, as we reflect on the gift of Jesus, let us come to Him with hearts full of gratitude, knowing that He is the Bread of Life who satisfies, sustains, and saves.

# Chapter 23 – Powerful Promise of Hope

In "O Come, Let Us Adore Him: A Christmas Devotional," we are reminded of the incredible truth that Christ in us is the Hope of Glory, a divine promise that fills our lives with hope, purpose, and a future beyond anything we can imagine. This hope is not a fleeting wish or a distant dream; it is a powerful reality grounded in the presence of Jesus within us, a promise that as we walk with Him, we are being prepared for the glory of eternity. "Christ in you, the hope of glory" (Colossians 1:27) speaks of a profound mystery, the amazing gift that the Savior of the world dwells in our hearts, transforming us from the inside out, filling us with His love, and guiding us toward an eternal glory that He has promised to those who believe. This hope is our anchor, giving us the strength to endure, the courage to press forward, and the assurance that God's purposes for us are good, even in the face of challenges. "Blessed be the God and Father of our Lord Jesus Christ, which according to his abundant mercy hath begotten us again unto a lively hope by the resurrection of Jesus Christ from the dead" (1 Peter 1:3). The hope we have in Jesus is alive, active, and enduring; it is a hope that cannot be shaken by the trials of life or the doubts of our hearts. This hope is rooted in the promise of eternal life, a glorious future where we will be with Him forever, experiencing the fullness of His love and the joy of His presence.

The Hope of Glory is a gift that transforms our present and our future, a reminder that our lives are part of a bigger story, one that leads us into the very presence of God. This hope is not dependent on our circumstances but on the unchanging character of God, who has promised to be with us, to guide us, and to bring us to a place of eternal joy. "For I know the thoughts that I think toward you, saith the Lord, thoughts of peace, and not of evil, to give you an expected end" (Jeremiah 29:11). The promise of God's presence in our lives fills us with peace, knowing that He has a plan for us, a future filled with hope and glory. This hope is a light in our darkness, a joy in our sorrow, and a strength in our weakness. It reminds us that we are never alone, that Jesus is with us, guiding us toward a future that is secure in His love and grace. In Christ, we have a hope that is unbreakable, a promise that is eternal, and a glory that awaits us beyond this life.

With Christ in us, we can face each day with confidence, knowing that His presence is our assurance, and His promises are our foundation. "Now the God of hope fill you with all joy and peace in believing, that ye may abound in hope, through the power of the Holy Ghost" (Romans 15:13). The joy and peace that come from believing in Jesus are evidence of this hope within us, a hope that abounds, overflows, and fills every corner of our lives. This hope is not just for the future; it is a present reality, a gift that empowers us to live with purpose, to love with compassion, and to walk in faith. It is the knowledge that God is working in us, shaping us into the image of His Son, and preparing us for the glory that awaits. As we hold onto this hope, we are strengthened by His grace, renewed by His Spirit, and filled with a joy that nothing in this world can take away.

The Hope of Glory assures us that our lives are valuable, that we are loved beyond measure, and that God's plans for us are filled with promise. "For our light affliction, which is but for a moment, worketh for us a far more exceeding and eternal weight of glory" (2 Corinthians 4:17). The challenges we face, the struggles we endure, and the pain we experience are not in vain; they are preparing us for a glory that outweighs them all, a glory that is eternal and magnificent. This hope gives us perspective, helping us to see beyond the temporary trials of this world and to focus on the eternal promises of God. In Jesus, we have a future that is secure, a glory that is promised, and a love that is everlasting. This hope is our source of joy, our reason for celebration, and our assurance that God is with us every step of the way, leading us toward a future that is filled with His glory.

As we embrace the Hope of Glory, we are called to live as people of hope, to reflect the love and grace of Jesus in all that we do, and to share this hope with those around us. "But sanctify the Lord God in your hearts: and be ready always to give an answer to every man that asketh you a reason of the hope that is in you" (1 Peter 3:15). The hope we have in Christ is a gift to be shared, a light to be spread, and a truth to be proclaimed. As we live with this hope, we become witnesses of God's love, messengers of His grace, and reflections of His glory. This hope is a gift that grows as we share it, a joy that deepens as we give it away, and a promise that strengthens as we live it out. In Jesus, we find the courage to face each day, the strength to overcome every challenge, and the assurance that our lives are part of a greater story, one that leads to eternal glory with Him.

This Christmas, as we reflect on the birth of Jesus, the Hope of Glory, may we be reminded that His presence in our lives is the greatest gift of all. Let us come before Him with hearts full of gratitude, embracing the hope He offers, and living each day in the light of His promises. For in Jesus, we have found a hope that endures, a love that never fails, and a future that is filled with glory.

# Chapter 24 – Pledge of a New Beginning

In "O Come, Let Us Adore Him: A Christmas Devotional," the wonder of Christmas brings us to the powerful truth that Jesus' birth marked the beginning of a New Covenant, a divine pledge of God's love and mercy toward us, offering reconciliation, redemption, and hope. When Jesus said, "This is my blood of the new testament, which is shed for many" (Mark 14:24), He was introducing a new relationship between God and humanity, one not based on our works or adherence to the old law, but on grace, faith, and the sacrifice of Christ. This New Covenant is God's unbreakable promise to draw us near, to forgive our sins, and to transform our hearts through His Spirit, opening the way for a relationship with Him that is intimate, eternal, and full of life. The birth of Jesus was the dawn of this new beginning, a moment when God came near to fulfill the prophecies and to offer us the greatest gift of all: His presence, His love, and His promise of eternal life. "For this is the covenant that I will make with the house of Israel after those days, saith the Lord; I will put my laws into their mind, and write them in their hearts: and I will be to them a God, and they shall be to me a people" (Hebrews 8:10). This is a covenant not written on tablets of stone but on the tender walls of our hearts, where God Himself plants His truth, His guidance, and His love, leading us into a life of joy and obedience that flows from within.

The New Covenant, sealed in Jesus' blood, is a divine pledge of forgiveness and grace, a covenant that promises to remember our sins no more and to cleanse us from all unrighteousness. "For I will be merciful to their unrighteousness, and their sins and their iniquities will I remember no more" (Hebrews 8:12). In Jesus, we find freedom from the guilt and shame that once separated us from God; we are made new, washed clean, and welcomed into His presence without fear or condemnation. His birth, life, death, and resurrection are all woven into this New Covenant, each a testament to His love and a reminder that He has done everything necessary for our salvation. We do not earn this relationship by our own merit; it is a gift, a promise that God has kept for us, fulfilling every requirement, bridging every gap, and opening every door so that we might walk freely in His grace. This is the joy of Christmas—that through Jesus, we are now children of the promise, heirs of His glory, and partakers in the divine nature, not by our works but by His love.

Through the New Covenant, Jesus reconciles us to God, restoring the broken relationship between humanity and our Creator, a relationship marred by sin yet redeemed through His blood. "And all things are of God, who hath reconciled us to himself by Jesus Christ" (2 Corinthians 5:18). This reconciliation is complete and perfect, bringing us peace with God and the joy of knowing that nothing can separate us from His love. Jesus stands as our mediator, the one who intercedes on our behalf, the one who opens the way for us to approach God with boldness and confidence, knowing that we are loved, accepted, and held secure in His grace. This New Covenant is a covenant of peace, a pledge that God will be our Father and that we will be His children forever. "For ye are all the children of God by faith in Christ Jesus" (Galatians 3:26). Through faith in Jesus, we step into this relationship, receiving His love, trusting in His promises, and walking in the assurance that we are His, now and forever.

The New Covenant also brings with it the indwelling of the Holy Spirit, God's own presence living within us, guiding, comforting, and empowering us to live in His will. "And I will pray the Father, and he shall give you another Comforter, that he may abide with you for ever" (John 14:16). The Holy Spirit is God's gift to us, a constant companion who reminds us of Jesus' words, teaches us all things, and fills our hearts with His love. This is the pledge of the New Covenant—that God Himself is with us, not just around us but within us, transforming us from the inside out, making us more like Jesus each day. The Spirit strengthens us in our weakness, gives us wisdom in our confusion, and brings us peace in our trials, assuring us that we are never alone. Through the Spirit, we are empowered to live out the life that Jesus has called us to, a life of love, joy, peace, and righteousness, reflecting His light to a world in need.

The New Covenant invites us to live in the freedom of grace, a life no longer bound by the law but inspired by love. "Stand fast therefore in the liberty wherewith Christ hath made us free" (Galatians 5:1). This freedom is not a license to sin but a call to live in holiness, to walk in the Spirit, and to bear the fruit of a life that is rooted in Jesus. Under the New Covenant, we are called to a life of love, not out of obligation but out of gratitude for all that He has done for us. We serve Him not to earn His favor but because we are deeply loved and completely accepted. This covenant liberates us from the weight of the law, replacing it with the joy of relationship, a relationship that fills our lives with purpose, peace, and joy.

As we celebrate the birth of Jesus, we remember that He is the fulfillment of the New Covenant, the embodiment of God's promises, the one who makes all things new. This Christmas, may we embrace the gift of His covenant, rejoicing in the love that came down to bring us hope, salvation, and eternal life. Let us adore Him, the one who has pledged Himself to us forever, who has written His love on our hearts, and who calls us His own. In Jesus, we have found our Savior, our Friend, and our Lord, the one who will never leave us nor forsake us. This is the hope and joy of Christmas—the promise of a New Covenant, the assurance of God's love, and the gift of His grace.

# Chapter 25 - Prince of Eternal Life

In "O Come, Let Us Adore Him: A Christmas Devotional," we are invited to celebrate Jesus, the Prince of Life, who came to earth to offer us not only a glimpse of God's love but the gift of life itself, abundant and eternal. The title "Prince of Life" speaks of Jesus as the one who holds the power of life in His hands, the one who, by His sacrifice and resurrection, has conquered death and opened the way for us to live forever with Him. "And killed the Prince of life, whom God hath raised from the dead" (Acts 3:15) reminds us that even though Jesus faced the darkest hour on the cross, death could not hold Him, and He rose in victory, proving that He is indeed the Lord of life, the giver of eternal hope to all who believe. Jesus, as the Prince of Life, is not only our Savior but also the very source of every breath, the one who gives meaning, purpose, and vitality to our existence. He is the light that shines in our darkness, the love that fills our hearts, and the joy that sustains us through every trial. "In him was life; and the life was the light of men" (John 1:4). Jesus doesn't just offer life; He is life, a life that is vibrant, joyful, and everlasting, a life that flows from the heart of God to each one of us who calls on His name.

The Prince of Life came to give us a new beginning, to offer a life that is free from the chains of sin and filled with His presence, His guidance, and His peace. "I am come that they might have life, and that they might have it more abundantly" (John 10:10). This abundant life is not limited to material blessings but is an overflow of joy, love, and contentment that springs from knowing Jesus personally. He fills our hearts with His love, His peace, and His hope, transforming us from the inside out. In Jesus, we find a life that is meaningful and fulfilling, a life that is centered on God's love and grounded in His promises. He leads us beside still waters, restores our souls, and walks with us through every valley, assuring us that we are never alone. This life in Jesus is a promise that we can hold on to, a joy that sustains us, and a hope that points us toward eternity with Him.

As the Prince of Life, Jesus offers eternal life, a life that does not end with physical death but continues forever in His presence. "For God so loved the world, that he gave his only begotten Son, that whosoever believeth in him should not perish, but have everlasting life" (John 3:16). Through Jesus, we are given the gift of eternal life, a promise that we will live forever with Him in a place where there is no more pain, no more sorrow, and no more death. This eternal life is the ultimate expression of God's love, a life that is filled with joy, peace, and the presence of God. It is a life that transcends the trials and struggles of this world, a life that is secure in the hands of our Savior, the one who conquered death and offers us the promise of resurrection. The Prince of Life has opened the door to eternity, inviting us to experience a life that is rich, full, and everlasting.

The life that Jesus offers is a life of freedom, a life where we are no longer bound by fear, guilt, or shame, but are free to live in His grace and walk in His truth. "If the Son therefore shall make you free, ye shall be free indeed" (John 8:36). In Jesus, we are free to be who God created us to be, free to live without fear of condemnation, free to love others as He has loved us. This freedom is a gift that fills our lives with joy and gives us the courage to face each day with hope. It is a freedom that comes from knowing that we are loved, accepted, and cherished by God, a freedom that allows us to walk in His light and to share His love with the world. This life of freedom is a life of purpose, a life where we are called to be His hands and feet, sharing the good news of His love and bringing hope to those who are lost.

The Prince of Life is not only our Savior but also our guide, the one who leads us on a path of righteousness, the one who teaches us to walk in His ways and to live in His love. "I am the way, the truth, and the life: no man cometh unto the Father, but by me" (John 14:6). Jesus is our way to the Father, our source of truth, and the very life we seek. In Him, we find direction, purpose, and fulfillment, a life that is guided by His wisdom and rooted in His truth. His words are a lamp unto our feet and a light unto our path, showing us the way to live a life that is pleasing to God and full of joy. He calls us to follow Him, to trust Him, and to live each day in the light of His love. This life in Jesus is a journey of faith, a journey that leads us closer to God and to the fullness of life that He has promised.

As we celebrate the birth of the Prince of Life, we are reminded that His coming is a gift that brings life to all who receive Him. Jesus is the light that shines in our darkness, the love that fills our hearts, and the hope that sustains us through every trial. His life is a promise of joy, peace, and purpose, a life that is grounded in His love and filled with His grace. This Christmas, may we come to Jesus, the Prince of Life, with hearts full of gratitude, embracing the life He offers and walking in the light of His love.

# Chapter 26 – Profound Offering of Redemption

In "O Come, Let Us Adore Him: A Christmas Devotional," the beauty of Christmas reveals the incredible depth of Jesus' love through His sacrifice for our sins, a sacrifice that brought forgiveness, redemption, and reconciliation with God. As we reflect on the birth of Christ, we remember that He came to earth not only to live among us but ultimately to die for us, bearing our sins and paying the price we could never pay. "But God commendeth his love toward us, in that, while we were yet sinners, Christ died for us" (Romans 5:8). This verse shows us the heart of God, a heart filled with compassion and mercy, choosing to love us even when we were lost in sin. Jesus, the spotless Lamb, took upon Himself the weight of all our transgressions, offering Himself as a perfect sacrifice, so that we could stand forgiven and cleansed in God's presence. His coming was an act of pure grace, a gift that reached beyond our brokenness and sin to bring us into the embrace of the Father's love. "For he hath made him to be sin for us, who knew no sin; that we might be made the righteousness of God in him" (2 Corinthians 5:21). Jesus became the substitute for our sins, taking our place on the cross, and in doing so, He gave us the gift of His righteousness, covering us with His grace and allowing us to be made whole.

The sacrifice of Jesus is a reminder of the cost of love, a love that would stop at nothing to bring us back to God. "Greater love hath no man than this, that a man lay down his life for his friends" (John 15:13). Jesus laid down His life willingly, embracing the cross so that we could know the depth of His love and the reality of God's mercy. His death was not the end but the beginning of a new relationship between God and humanity, a relationship built on forgiveness, grace, and eternal hope. Through His sacrifice, we are invited to experience a life that is free from the burden of sin, a life filled with His peace and anchored in His promises. This sacrifice was an act of divine love, a love that looked beyond our faults and saw our need for a Savior, a love that reached into our darkness and brought us into the light of God's presence. "Herein is love, not that we loved God, but that he loved us, and sent his Son to be the propitiation for our sins" (1 John 4:10). The word "propitiation" means that Jesus satisfied the demands of justice, that He absorbed the punishment for our sins so that we could be forgiven. He paid a price we could never pay, giving us a gift we could never earn.

Through Jesus' sacrifice, we are reconciled to God, restored to a relationship that was once broken by sin but is now healed by His love. "And all things are of God, who hath reconciled us to himself by Jesus Christ" (2 Corinthians 5:18). This reconciliation means that we are no longer separated from God; we are brought near, invited to call Him Father, and assured of His love. Jesus opened the way for us to experience a closeness with God that fills our hearts with peace, joy, and security. This is the wonder of Christmas—that God Himself would come near, not to condemn but to save, not to judge but to redeem. In Jesus, we see the face of God's mercy, a mercy that reaches us in our weakness, lifts us from our brokenness, and restores us to His embrace.

The sacrifice of Jesus is also our invitation to new life, a life that is no longer bound by sin but filled with His Spirit, a life that reflects His love and bears witness to His grace. "Therefore if any man be in Christ, he is a new creature: old things are passed away; behold, all things are become new" (2 Corinthians 5:17). Through His death and resurrection, Jesus offers us the gift of transformation, a chance to leave behind our past and step into a future filled with His hope. In Him, we are made new, washed clean, and given a purpose that is rooted in His love and guided by His Spirit. This new life is a gift of grace, a life that is not earned by our efforts but received through faith in His sacrifice. We are reminded that because of His love, we are forgiven, accepted, and called to live in the freedom of His grace.

Jesus' sacrifice is the ultimate expression of God's heart, a heart that would go to any length to save us, to rescue us from sin, and to give us the gift of eternal life. "For the wages of sin is death; but the gift of God is eternal life through Jesus Christ our Lord" (Romans 6:23). This gift of eternal life is a promise that death is not the end, that in Jesus, we have hope that reaches beyond this life and into eternity. His sacrifice assures us that we are loved with an everlasting love, a love that conquered death and promises us a future filled with His presence. This Christmas, as we reflect on the birth of Jesus, we are reminded that He came to give us more than just a moment of peace; He came to give us eternal life, a life that is secure in His love and filled with His joy.

The gift of Jesus' sacrifice calls us to live in gratitude, to embrace the grace He offers, and to walk in the freedom of His love. As we receive His forgiveness, we are invited to extend that same grace to others, to be ambassadors of His love, and to share the message of His sacrifice with a world in need. "And be ye kind one to another, tenderhearted, forgiving one another, even as God for Christ's sake hath forgiven you" (Ephesians 4:32). Jesus' sacrifice teaches us to live with compassion, to forgive as we have been forgiven, and to love as we have been loved. This is the call of Christmas—to let His love transform our hearts, to let His grace fill our lives, and to let His sacrifice be the foundation of our faith.

In Jesus, we find a Savior who not only understands our struggles but has walked through them, who has faced every temptation and trial, and who has overcome it all on our behalf. His sacrifice is our hope, our assurance, and our reason for joy. This Christmas, as we come to adore Him, let us remember the price He paid, the love He gave, and the life He offers to all who believe. For in Jesus, we have found the gift of forgiveness, the promise of reconciliation, and the hope of eternal life.

# Chapter 27 - Perfect Grace

In "O Come, Let Us Adore Him: A Christmas Devotional," the beauty of God's grace is revealed fully through the gift of Jesus, a grace that forgives, heals, and brings us into a relationship with our Creator. The birth of Jesus signifies the arrival of a divine pardon, a grace that reaches every heart, forgives every sin, and offers us salvation. "For the grace of God that bringeth salvation hath appeared to all men" (Titus 2:11). This is a grace that transcends our flaws, our failures, and our fears, embracing us with a love that is unearned and undeserved, a love that flows from the heart of God directly to each of us. God's grace through Jesus is the ultimate gift, the good news of forgiveness and reconciliation, a promise that no matter where we have been or what we have done, we are welcomed into His love, redeemed by His mercy, and covered by His grace. This is not a grace that demands perfection but meets us in our weakness, a grace that lifts us up when we fall, that forgives us when we stray, and that assures us of His love despite our imperfections. "But God, who is rich in mercy, for his great love wherewith he loved us, even when we were dead in sins, hath quickened us together with Christ, (by grace ye are saved)" (Ephesians 2:4-5). This grace is a reminder that our salvation is not based on our works or our worthiness but solely on the love and kindness of a God who chooses us, redeems us, and makes us His own.

Through Jesus, we experience a grace that breaks every chain, a grace that frees us from the bondage of sin and opens the door to a life of purpose, joy, and peace. "Being justified freely by his grace through the redemption that is in Christ Jesus" (Romans 3:24). In Jesus, we find forgiveness for our past, strength for our present, and hope for our future. This grace is a daily reminder that we are loved, accepted, and held secure in God's hands, not because of what we do but because of who He is. Jesus' coming is a declaration that God's grace is for everyone, reaching every corner of the earth, every broken heart, and every weary soul. His grace is like a river, constantly flowing, cleansing, and renewing, bringing life and hope to all who believe. This Christmas, as we reflect on the birth of our Savior, we are reminded that His grace is more than enough, that His love is steadfast, and that His mercy is new every morning.

God's grace is a gift that transforms us, changing the way we see ourselves and the way we see others. "Let us therefore come boldly unto the throne of grace, that we may obtain mercy, and find grace to help in time of need" (Hebrews 4:16). Through Jesus, we are invited to come boldly to God, to approach Him with confidence, knowing that we are loved and accepted, that His grace covers all our sins, and that His love casts out all fear. This is the grace that comforts us in our sorrow, strengthens us in our weakness, and fills us with peace in times of trouble. It is a grace that assures us of God's presence, a grace that reminds us that we are never alone, and a grace that promises to carry us through every season of life. In Jesus, we find the grace that meets us where we are but does not leave us there, a grace that lifts us, renews us, and leads us into the fullness of life that God has prepared for us.

The grace of God, revealed through Jesus, is a grace that calls us to live in love, to extend the same forgiveness and kindness that we have received. "And be ye kind one to another, tenderhearted, forgiving one another, even as God for Christ's sake hath forgiven you" (Ephesians 4:32). As recipients of His grace, we are called to be ambassadors of His love, to show compassion, to forgive freely, and to love deeply. This grace is not something we keep to ourselves but something we are meant to share, a light that shines through us, reflecting the love of Jesus to a world in need. His grace teaches us to live with humility, to serve others with joy, and to walk in a way that honors Him. It is a grace that changes us from the inside out, shaping our hearts to be more like His, filling our lives with His peace, and guiding our steps in His truth.

As we celebrate Christmas, we are reminded that God's grace is not just a concept but a person—Jesus, who came to bring us life, hope, and a future. "For ye know the grace of our Lord Jesus Christ, that, though he was rich, yet for your sakes he became poor, that ye through his poverty might be rich" (2 Corinthians 8:9). Jesus left the glory of heaven, humbled Himself, and came to earth, bringing with Him the fullness of God's grace. His birth is the beginning of a story of redemption, a story that tells us that we are loved beyond measure, that we are valued beyond words, and that we are held in the hands of a God who will never let us go. His grace is the reason for our hope, the source of our strength, and the foundation of our faith. This Christmas, let us come to adore Him, the one who is full of grace and truth, the one who has come to give us life and life more abundantly.

In Jesus, we find a grace that is sufficient for every need, a grace that carries us through every challenge, and a grace that reminds us that we are His beloved children. This grace is a gift that we cannot earn, a love that we cannot deserve, and a hope that we cannot lose. Let us rest in His grace, trust in His promises, and rejoice in the gift of His love.

# Chapter 28 – Passionate Love

In "O Come, Let Us Adore Him: A Christmas Devotional," we are invited to reflect on the profound truth of God's love made known to us through the birth of Jesus, a love that is deep, sacrificial, and unchanging. Christmas is the story of love beyond measure, a love that moved the heart of God to send His only Son to live among us, to die for us, and to open the way for us to be reconciled to Him. "For God so loved the world, that he gave his only begotten Son, that whosoever believeth in him should not perish, but have everlasting life" (John 3:16). This verse reveals the incredible passion of God's heart for humanity, a passion that would lead Him to give up His most precious gift, His Son, so that we could experience life, hope, and joy. God's love is not passive; it is an active, relentless love that pursues us, reaches out to us, and meets us in our darkest moments. His love is a love that gives all, sacrifices all, and holds nothing back. In Jesus, we see the embodiment of this divine love, a love that chose to walk among us, to experience our pain, and to carry our burdens. This is a love that does not turn away but comes close, a love that is willing to bear our sins, to heal our wounds, and to bring us into the light of God's presence.

The love of God, made known through Jesus, is a love that transforms, heals, and redeems. "But God commendeth his love toward us, in that, while we were yet sinners, Christ died for us" (Romans 5:8). This love is not based on our worthiness but on God's grace, a love that reaches out to us even when we are lost, broken, and far from Him. Jesus came not to condemn but to save, not to judge but to offer mercy, showing us that God's love is greater than our failures and more powerful than our fears. In Him, we find forgiveness for our sins, a new beginning, and a love that restores our hearts and brings peace to our souls. God's love is a love that meets us where we are but does not leave us there; it is a love that lifts us, that calls us higher, and that fills our lives with purpose. Through Jesus, we are given the gift of God's love, a love that changes everything, a love that fills the empty places in our hearts and gives us the courage to live with hope and joy.

As we celebrate the birth of Jesus, we are reminded that His coming is the ultimate display of God's love for humanity, a love that is faithful, steadfast, and eternal. "Herein is love, not that we loved God, but that he loved us, and sent his Son to be the propitiation for our sins" (1 John 4:10). This love is a love that goes beyond our understanding, a love that gives all and asks for nothing in return, a love that sees us in our brokenness and chooses us anyway. God's love is a love that is patient, kind, and enduring, a love that never fails and never fades. In Jesus, we see the heart of God, a heart that is filled with compassion, mercy, and grace, a heart that longs to be close to us, to heal us, and to make us whole. This is the love that was born in a manger, a love that would grow to carry the cross, and a love that would rise again, victorious over sin and death.

The love of God, revealed in Jesus, is a love that calls us to come near, to trust in His goodness, and to rest in His grace. "Behold, what manner of love the Father hath bestowed upon us, that we should be called the sons of God" (1 John 3:1). Through Jesus, we are not only forgiven but welcomed into God's family, given the privilege to call Him Father and to live in the security of His love. This love is a love that surrounds us, that holds us, and that never lets us go. It is a love that whispers to our hearts in moments of doubt, reminding us that we are His, that we are loved, and that we are never alone. God's love is a love that casts out fear, a love that fills us with peace, and a love that gives us strength to face each day with confidence and hope. In Jesus, we have found a love that is strong, unbreakable, and everlasting, a love that stands as a constant reminder that we are cherished, valued, and held in the arms of a loving Savior.

This Christmas, as we reflect on the birth of Jesus, let us be reminded that His coming is the greatest gift of love, a gift that brings light to our darkness, hope to our despair, and joy to our hearts. In Jesus, we see the lengths to which God would go to bring us back to Himself, the depth of His love, and the beauty of His grace. "For I am persuaded, that neither death, nor life, nor angels, nor principalities, nor powers, nor things present, nor things to come... shall be able to separate us from the love of God, which is in Christ Jesus our Lord" (Romans 8:38-39). This love is a love that cannot be shaken, a love that holds us through every storm, and a love that promises to be with us always. In

Jesus, we have found a love that is perfect, a love that is complete, and a love that brings peace to our souls.

As we adore Him, the one who came to reveal God's love, may our hearts be filled with gratitude, our lives be changed by His grace, and our spirits be renewed by the hope that His love brings. This is the love that gives us life, the love that calls us His own, and the love that assures us of His presence, now and forever. In Jesus, we find the heart of God, a heart that is for us, a heart that is with us, and a heart that will never let us go.

# Chapter 29 – Priceless Redemption

In "O Come, Let Us Adore Him: A Christmas Devotional," we are invited to reflect on the miraculous truth of our redemption through Jesus Christ, a gift beyond measure that brings us back to God, washes away our sins, and frees us from the chains of death. Christmas is the celebration of our Redeemer's arrival, the One who came to buy us back from sin, a perfect and priceless purchase made through His precious blood. "In whom we have redemption through his blood, the forgiveness of sins, according to the riches of his grace" (Ephesians 1:7). In Jesus, we see the heart of God reaching out to us, choosing to sacrifice everything so that we might be brought back to Him. Jesus' coming was not just to live among us but to redeem us, a divine plan set from the beginning to rescue humanity from darkness and bring us into His marvelous light. His sacrifice was a costly one, showing us just how valuable we are in the eyes of God. This redemption means that we are no longer defined by our failures, our past, or our mistakes; we are made new, cleansed, and welcomed as His beloved children. Through His love, we have been redeemed, forgiven, and set free, not because of anything we have done, but solely because of His grace.

Jesus, as our Redeemer, willingly took upon Himself the weight of our sins, bearing the punishment that was ours, and paying the price that we could never pay. "For ye are bought with a price: therefore glorify God in your body, and in your spirit, which are God's" (1 Corinthians 6:20). He purchased us with His own life, giving everything so that we might have life eternal. This redemption was not a mere transaction but a passionate, purposeful act of love, one that reached beyond heaven's glory and entered into our brokenness to heal and restore. In Jesus, we find a Redeemer who loves us so deeply that He would face death itself to bring us back to God. His love is stronger than death, His grace greater than our sins, and His mercy a shelter for our weary souls. In Him, we are no longer slaves to fear, sin, or shame; we are redeemed, set free, and given a new identity as sons and daughters of the King.

The redemption we have in Jesus is not only a release from the power of sin but an invitation to live in the fullness of His grace, a life transformed by His Spirit and filled with His peace. "For as much as ye know that ye were not redeemed with corruptible things, as silver and gold, from your vain conversation received by tradition from your fathers; but with the precious blood of Christ, as of a lamb without blemish and without spot" (1 Peter 1:18-19). Jesus' blood, pure and undefiled, is the price of our redemption, a gift that could never be matched or measured. He has paid it all, covering every sin, every failure, and every weakness, drawing us near to God with a love that cannot be shaken. This redemption means that we are held in God's grace, wrapped in His mercy, and secure in His love, a promise that our sins are forgiven and that we are forever His.

Through His redemption, Jesus brings us peace, a peace that calms our fears, heals our hearts, and reminds us that we are never alone. "And having made peace through the blood of his cross, by him to reconcile all things unto himself" (Colossians 1:20). This peace is the result of our reconciliation with God, a restoration of the relationship that sin had broken but grace has mended. In Jesus, we have found our true home, a place of belonging, love, and acceptance. His redemption is our assurance that we are loved beyond measure, cherished beyond words, and held in His hands, safe and secure. We are reminded that we are no longer defined by our past, no longer condemned by our mistakes, and no longer bound by fear. In Jesus, we are redeemed, restored, and renewed, filled with the hope of His love and the joy of His salvation.

As we celebrate Christmas, let us remember the incredible gift of our redemption, a gift that brings us freedom, forgiveness, and a future filled with hope. "Let the redeemed of the Lord say so, whom he hath redeemed from the hand of the enemy" (Psalm 107:2). This redemption is our reason to rejoice, our hope in times of trial, and our strength in moments of weakness. In Jesus, we find a Redeemer who is always with us, guiding us, comforting us, and reminding us that we are His forever. This Christmas may our hearts be filled with gratitude for the love of our Redeemer, the one who came to seek and to save, the one who gave His life to bring us life, and the one who rose again to give us a hope that endures.

In Jesus, we find the redemption that changes everything, a love that fills every empty place, a grace that lifts every burden, and a joy that cannot be taken away. He is our Redeemer, our Savior, and our Friend, the one who holds us close, carries us through, and promises to be with us always. His love is our redemption, His grace our strength, and His peace our comfort. This Christmas, let us come and adore Him, the Redeemer of our souls, the one who has purchased us with His love, and the one who calls us His own. In Jesus, we are redeemed, forever loved, and forever free.

# Chapter 30 - Perpetual Reign

In "O Come, Let Us Adore Him: A Christmas Devotional," we celebrate the truth that Jesus was born to reign as the eternal King, a King whose power, love, and majesty reach beyond our understanding, filling us with hope, joy, and reverence. The birth of Jesus in a humble manger is the beginning of a reign that knows no end, a kingdom that is not of this world but one that brings peace, justice, and love to all who believe. "And he shall reign over the house of Jacob for ever; and of his kingdom there shall be no end" (Luke 1:33). His reign is marked by righteousness and compassion, a rule that transforms lives and brings light into the darkest places. Jesus, our King, was not born to wear a crown of earthly riches but one of heavenly glory, a King who serves, who loves, and who sacrifices Himself for His people. He is the King of Kings and Lord of Lords, whose name is above every name, whose throne is established in heaven, and whose power is unmatched. "Wherefore God also hath highly exalted him, and given him a name which is above every name" (Philippians 2:9). The power of His kingdom is not rooted in the strength of armies or the wealth of nations but in the love, mercy, and grace of God, a kingdom where peace reigns and justice flow like a river.

Jesus came to establish a kingdom that brings hope to the hopeless, freedom to the captive, and rest to the weary. His reign is one of compassion and kindness, reaching out to the lost and drawing them into His embrace. "Come unto me, all ye that labour and are heavy laden, and I will give you rest" (Matthew 11:28). In His kingdom, every heart finds peace, every soul finds purpose, and every life finds worth. Jesus reigns as the Good Shepherd, caring for His flock, guiding us in paths of righteousness, and leading us beside still waters. His kingdom is a refuge for the broken, a home for the lonely, and a place of healing for the wounded. This is a kingdom not built by human hands but by the hands of a loving Savior who gave His life so that we might live. "For unto us a child is born, unto us a son is given: and the government shall be upon his shoulder" (Isaiah 9:6). Jesus is not only our Savior but our eternal King, a King who rules with wisdom and justice, a King who knows us by name and calls us His own.

In Jesus, we find a King who understands our struggles, who walks with us through every trial, and who offers us His peace in every storm. "Peace I leave with you, my peace I give unto you: not as the world giveth, give I unto you. Let not your heart be troubled, neither let it be afraid" (John 14:27). His reign brings a peace that surpasses all understanding, a joy that fills our hearts, and a hope that cannot be shaken. As we look to Jesus, the King born in Bethlehem, we see the fulfillment of God's promises, the One who was prophesied to come and bring salvation to His people. He is the Prince of Peace, the Light of the World, and the Hope of Glory. His kingdom is not one of earthly power but of heavenly love, a kingdom that invites all to come and find rest, forgiveness, and eternal life. "For the kingdom of God is not meat and drink; but righteousness, and peace, and joy in the Holy Ghost" (Romans 14:17).

The reign of Jesus is eternal, unending, and unbreakable. No power on earth or in heaven can overthrow His kingdom, no force can weaken His rule, and no darkness can diminish His light. "Of the increase of his government and peace there shall be no end" (Isaiah 9:7). He reigns forever, a King who conquered death, defeated sin, and opened the way to eternal life for all who believe. Jesus is the Alpha and the Omega, the beginning and the end, the One who holds all things together by the word of His power. His kingdom is a kingdom of love, a kingdom that will one day be fully realized when He returns in glory. As we celebrate His birth, we look forward to His coming again, when every knee shall bow and every tongue confess that Jesus Christ is Lord, to the glory of God the Father. "And I heard a great voice out of heaven saying, Behold, the tabernacle of God is with men, and he will dwell with them, and they shall be his people, and God himself shall be with them, and be their God" (Revelation 21:3).

This Christmas, let us adore our King, the one who left the glory of heaven to walk among us, to know our pain, and to offer us His love. Let us bow before Him, acknowledging His lordship, and giving Him the praise and honor that He deserves. Jesus, our King, is not distant or unapproachable; He is near, He is compassionate, and He is full of grace. His kingdom is here, within us, bringing transformation to our hearts and lives. As we come to Jesus, we enter into a relationship with the King of Kings, a relationship that fills us with His power, equips us with His peace, and sends us out to be ambassadors of His love. In Jesus, we find a kingdom that cannot be shaken, a kingdom that invites us to live with purpose, to walk in faith, and to share His love with the world. Let us come and adore Him, our reigning King, whose kingdom is forever, whose power is infinite, and whose love is everlasting.

# Chapter 31 – Profound Promise

In "O Come, Let Us Adore Him: A Christmas Devotional," we celebrate the miraculous birth of our Savior, the one who came to bring salvation, hope, and peace to all who believe. The birth of Jesus is the fulfillment of God's promise, a moment that changed the course of history and offers us eternal life. "For unto you is born this day in the city of David a Saviour, which is Christ the Lord" (Luke 2:11). Jesus, born in a humble manger, is the Savior who brings peace to our troubled hearts, a light that shines in our darkest nights, and a hope that reaches into eternity. His coming is the ultimate expression of God's love, a gift of grace that is freely offered to everyone who places their trust in Him. The birth of Jesus is more than a story; it is the beginning of our salvation, the arrival of the One who would live, die, and rise again so that we might have life. "And she shall bring forth a son, and thou shalt call his name Jesus: for he shall save his people from their sins" (Matthew 1:21). Jesus came to save us from the power of sin and death, to set us free from the burdens that weigh us down, and to offer us a relationship with God that is full of joy, peace, and purpose. This is the good news of Christmas—that God sent His only Son into the world to be our Savior, to heal our brokenness, and to bring us back to Him.

The birth of Jesus brings a peace that the world cannot give, a peace that calms our fears, soothes our sorrows, and fills our hearts with hope. "Peace I leave with you, my peace I give unto you: not as the world giveth, give I unto you. Let not your heart be troubled, neither let it be afraid" (John 14:27). His peace is not dependent on our circumstances but is rooted in His presence, a peace that sustains us through every trial and assures us that we are never alone. In Jesus, we find a peace that surpasses all understanding, a peace that guards our hearts and minds, and a peace that invites us to rest in the love of our Savior. The angels proclaimed this peace to the shepherds, declaring, "Glory to God in the highest, and on earth peace, good will toward men" (Luke 2:14). This peace is a gift from God, a reminder that He is with us, that He is for us, and that His love is unchanging. Jesus is our Prince of Peace, the one who calms the storms in our lives and fills us with a joy that is unshakable, a joy that springs from knowing that we are loved and held by the Creator of the universe.

The Savior's birth is an invitation to come and experience the grace of God, a grace that forgives, heals, and restores. "For by grace are ye saved through faith; and that not of yourselves: it is the gift of God" (Ephesians 2:8). This grace is a gift that we cannot earn, a love that we do not deserve, and a hope that we cannot lose. Jesus came to offer us a relationship with God that is based not on our own efforts but on His sacrifice, a relationship that is full of mercy, compassion, and acceptance. In Him, we find the forgiveness that sets us free, the love that fills our hearts, and the strength that carries us through every season. This Christmas, we are reminded that the Savior's birth is the beginning of our journey of faith, a journey that leads us to the cross, to the empty tomb, and to the hope of eternity with Him. "But God commendeth his love toward us, in that, while we were yet sinners, Christ died for us" (Romans 5:8). Jesus, our Savior, came to lay down His life for us, to bear our sins, and to bring us back to God. His birth is the start of a story of redemption, a story that assures us of God's love, a love that is constant, faithful, and everlasting.

In Jesus, we have a Savior who understands our struggles, who walks with us through our pain, and who offers us His comfort and strength. "For we have not an high priest which cannot be touched with the feeling of our infirmities; but was in all points tempted like as we are, yet without sin" (Hebrews 4:15). He is the Savior who knows our hearts, who sees our needs, and who meets us in our weakness. His love is a love that lifts us up, that fills us with hope, and that calls us to live with faith and courage. This Christmas, as we adore the newborn King, we are reminded that His love is for all people, that His grace is for everyone who believes, and that His peace is a promise we can hold on to. Jesus is the Savior of the world, the Light that shines in our darkness, and the Shepherd who leads us in paths of righteousness. His birth is a message of hope, a declaration of love, and an invitation to come and find rest for our souls.

The Savior's birth is a reminder that God is with us, that He is Emmanuel, and that His presence is our greatest treasure. "Behold, a virgin shall be with child, and shall bring forth a son, and they shall call his name Emmanuel, which being interpreted is, God with us" (Matthew 1:23). This is the miracle of

Christmas—that God Himself came to dwell among us, to walk in our shoes, and to show us the way to the Father. His presence is our peace, His love our comfort, and His grace our hope. In Jesus, we have found the One who satisfies our deepest longings, who heals our broken hearts, and who fills us with a joy that endures. This is the joy of Christmas—that the Savior has come, that He has conquered sin and death, and that He offers us a life that is full of purpose, meaning, and hope. "I am come that they might have life, and that they might have it more abundantly" (John 10:10). Jesus came to give us abundant life, a life that is rich in His love, overflowing with His grace, and anchored in His truth.

This Christmas, as we celebrate the birth of our Savior, let us come with hearts full of gratitude, bowing before Him in adoration, and receiving the peace that only He can give. Let us rejoice in the gift of His love, the promise of His salvation, and the hope of His return. Jesus is the Savior who was born for us, the King who reigns forever, and the Shepherd who guides us with His gentle hand. In Him, we find everything we need, a love that is steadfast, a peace that is perfect, and a hope that is eternal. The Savior is born, and because of Him, we have a reason to sing, a reason to hope, and a reason to live. Let us come and adore Him, Christ the Lord, our Savior, our Redeemer, and our Friend.—-

# Don't miss out!

Visit the website below and you can sign up to receive emails whenever Joshua Rhoades publishes a new book. There's no charge and no obligation.

https://books2read.com/r/B-A-AJLBB-ALVDF

**BOOKS 2 READ**

Connecting independent readers to independent writers.

Did you love *O Come, Let Us Adore Him- A Christmas Devotional*? Then you should read *David's Song Of Deliverance Praising God Through Every Storm*[1] by Joshua Rhoades!

[2]

"David's Song of Deliverance: Praising God Through Every Storm" takes readers on a powerful journey through the life of King David, one of the most iconic figures in the Bible. David's courage and unwavering faith were matched only by the intensity of his trials. He faced devastating challenges: being hunted by King Saul, enduring exile, betrayal, and relentless battles. Yet, in his darkest moments, David found refuge in God, and it was through those storms that his praise to the Lord soared the highest. His psalms, especially Psalm 34, reveal a heart that understood true deliverance doesn't come from escaping hardship, but from praising God through it.

This book peers into how David mastered the art of praising God in every season, particularly when faced with adversity. His life provides a timeless blueprint for how we, too, can lift our hearts in praise when surrounded by

---

1. https://books2read.com/u/mdaj7l

2. https://books2read.com/u/mdaj7l

chaos, fear, and uncertainty. David didn't shy away from expressing pain, but he always returned to one truth: God is his deliverer.

As we navigate our own personal storms—whether they be trials, emotional struggles, or spiritual battles—David's life shows us that praise is our anchor. This book offers practical insights from David's psalms, teaching us how praise shifts our focus from the storm to the One who commands it, bringing peace and deliverance.

9 7 9 8 2 2 7 9 7 7 2 1 2